Common Sense, Legal Sense and Nonsense About Divorce

Common Sense, Legal Sense and Nonsense About Divorce

Lenard Marlow, J.D.

To order additional copies of this book, contact:
Xlibris Corporation
1-888-795-4274
www.Xlibris.com
Orders@Xlibris.com
98059

CONTENTS

PART III
The Price That Is To Be Paid for Legal Nonsense

PART IV
Substituting Your Common Sense for Legal Nonsense

To Leslie

Whose sunshine brightens up my life, every day.

PREFACE

As anyone who has gone through a divorce will tell you, it is one of the most difficult experiences that anyone will be required to negotiate in their lives.

It is understandable, therefore, that divorcing husbands and wives will look for help. They will turn to friends and relatives for support. They will talk to co-workers who have gone through their own divorce. They will go on the internet to get information. And, of course, they will read books. That is why you are reading this book.

Unfortunately, the books that most people read do not help. They certainly do not solve their problems. Rather, they fill their heads with a lot of useless information. They also give them a great deal of misinformation. Worse, they send them off in a hundred different directions, going nowhere. Thus, instead of calming their fears, they end up only underscoring their anxiety. In short, they leave them more confused and more overwhelmed when they get done than they were when they began.

This book is not going to do that. Understandably, there will be a number of questions that you and your husband or wife will have to answer and decisions that you will have to make. There will also be problems that the two of you will have to solve. But, as I will argue, there is very little that you will need that you do not already have. That is your good judgment and the personal considerations that are important to you, which I will refer to as your *common sense*.

To be sure, your common sense will not always be enough. When that is the case, you will have to look to something else. For better or worse, there is only one place that you can turn, and that is the law, which I will refer to as getting legal information. In many instances turning to the law will help, and when it does, it will represent what I will call *legal sense.* All too often, however, turning to the law will not help. Rather than solve your problems as you have been led to believe, it will only leave you with problems. When it does that, the law does not represent legal sense. It represents what I will call *legal nonsense.*

It is important that you keep the distinction between legal sense and legal nonsense in mind. It is important that you do not make the mistake that so many divorcing husbands and wives do of confusing the two. If you do, you will take what is only legal nonsense and give it license to pass itself off as legal sense. Worse, you will allow legal nonsense to trump your common sense.

While this book will represent one sustained argument, I am not trying to prove anything. Rather, I am trying to get you to see something. It is what all of the talk that lawyers engage in, and all of the lofty abstractions that they forever invoke—about your *legal rights* and what is *fair* and *equitable*—disable you from being able to see. Your divorce does not leave you with a legal problem, as divorce lawyers would have you believe. It leaves you with personal and practical problems that simply have certain legal implications.

As you will find, my argument will be a very simple one. That being the case, you will not have had to go to law school to understand it. Since everything that I will tell you is nothing more than common sense, that is all that you will need. In fact, that is the simple message of this book. What you need most now is your common sense. All that you have to do is use it. It is important that you remember this. Your future well-being and that of your children depend upon it.

Part I

Common Sense

CHAPTER 1

Common Sense

If you are like most people, you do not know very much about the law. Nor do you understand how divorce lawyers employ the legal rules and procedures that they have been given or for what purpose. Nevertheless, more than somewhat overwhelmed by the prospect of your divorce, and more than a little fearful when it comes to the future, like most people your immediate reaction is to turn to lawyers and the law. You tend to see the law as a life line. You believe that if you grab hold of it and hang on to it, it will somehow save you.

That is the mistake that all too many people make. Taken in by the window dressing that divorce lawyers employ to sell their wares, they sanctify the law, put it on a pedestal, and place a halo around it. Miraculously, and in a way they do not know and have not given much thought to, they believe that the law will not only answer all of their questions and solve all of their problems, but also protect them. Moreover, they endow lawyers with the ability to somehow bring about this miracle, even though they have no idea just how they are going to do that.

Their common sense should be enough to tell them that this is not possible. Their experience should confirm it. Unfortunately, the unrealistic fantasy that they have created when it comes to the law, and the miraculous powers that they have endowed divorce lawyers with, has put their common sense to sleep and gotten them to ignore their experience. Both would tell them that running off to divorce lawyers will not solve their problems. Both would tell them that it is only going to make things worse.

Their common sense and experience would tell them something else, and that is that it is not going to be possible for their lawyers to deliver what they have led each of them to believe they have a right to expect. How could they when they have given them such different answers to the same questions? How could they when the pictures they have held up showing them what they have a right to expect—in a divorce lawyer's terms, what would represent a fair and equitable agreement—do not even resemble one another? How could they when it is all just talk?

The irony is that divorcing husbands and wives knows this. Why then do they ignore what they know? They make the mistake of attributing the madness that they see taking place in the lives of friends and relatives who have run off to divorce lawyers as being simply the inevitable by-product of their divorce rather than a consequence of how they have gone about concluding their marriage. They tell themselves that this is what all divorcing husbands and wives do and how they act. It isn't. It is only what they do and how they act when, having fantasized the law and unrealistically endowed lawyers with the power to perform miracles, they make the mistake of turning their lives over to them. It is only what happens when, rather than sitting down and answering the questions and solving the problems that they find themselves faced with in a responsible manner, they allow lawyers to take their lives and make a game of it. That is only because the first rule of the game their lawyers will play is that there are no rules. It is anything that the law will allow and, as they will quickly find, the law will allow a great deal.

Needless to say, this does not represent legal sense as divorce lawyers would have you believe. It is nothing but legal nonsense, and irresponsible nonsense at that. The problems that you now find yourself faced with are serious ones, far too serious to make a game of them. Again, your common sense is enough to tell you this. Fortunately, as countless husbands and wives have learned, it doesn't have to come to that. That is why you are reading this book. You don't want it to happen to you.

CHAPTER 2

A Silly Little Story That Isn't So Silly

I am going to start by telling you a story. I call it a silly little story that isn't so silly. It is the story of Mark, who is a manufacturer's representative, and Susan, who is a school teacher. They have been married for twelve years and have two children, ages eight and six. There have been serious problems in their marriage for some time as a result of which they have decided to divorce. Believing that their decision has left them with a legal problem, they have decided to consult with a lawyer, Justin Wright, and have made an appointment with him for that purpose.

When they arrived at Mr. Wright's office, he ushered them into his small library which was filled with shelves of law books on both sides. In the middle of the room was a small round conference table. To the side was a telephone stand with a telephone on it.

When they had all seated themselves, Mr. Wright turned to Mark and Susan and said: "I know this will surprise you, but I have been sitting here for the last twelve years waiting for the two of you to call me. Not that I knew you were going to divorce. How could I have known that? But since I have gone to law school and have a license to practice law, and must therefore have a head this big," Mr. Wright said, spreading his hands apart on each side of his head to emphasize the point, "it would never have occurred to me that the two of you would make any of the important decisions in your lives without first getting my good opinion. And I must tell you that it has been very lonely, and very ego deflating, to sit here, night after night, not hearing from you, and having the two of you just go about the business of your lives without first speaking to me."

"But it always amazes me," Mr. Wright continued, "how smart I suddenly become just because the two of you decide to change the direction of your lives—to divorce rather than to marry. You certainly didn't call me then, though I would have had a lot of good advice for you if you had. Now that you have decided to divorce, however, the phone never stops ringing. Neither of you would dare make a move without first getting my good opinion."

"And I want to congratulate you. I don't know what has taken you so long to call me," he went on, "but you were right to do so. After all, I do have a law degree and a license to practice law, and I do have a head this big," Mr. Wright continued, again spreading his hands apart for emphasis. "For example, I have spent years reading all of the cases in the books in this room which set forth what the law considers to be in the best interest of your children. I have also lectured on the subject and written extensively about it. In fact, I am considered to be an expert in the field. That being the case—and because I know that you only want what is best for your children—I think that the two of you should make the first decision in your divorce. Since neither of you are lawyers, I am clearly the only one here who is an expert when it come to what the law considers to be in your children's best interest. I therefore think that, from this point forward, I should make all of the important decisions in their lives."

"If I were to say anything that foolish," Mr. Wright went on, "if you had any sense, the two of you would get up and get out of here as quickly as you could, for you are obviously dealing with a madman. Someone who has never met your children, let alone raised them, seriously believes that he knows better than you do what is best for them. That is not legal sense. Your common sense is enough to tell you that. It is nothing but legal nonsense."

"You will excuse me," Mr. Wright went on. "You get it when it comes to your children, but you lose it when it comes to your money. Thus, you tell yourselves, 'Even if he does not know what is best for our children, since he did go to law school and since he does have a license to practice law, he must know what is best for our money.' I am sorry to disappoint you, but I don't. I didn't raise your children and I didn't make your money. I am not an expert when it comes to either."

"'But I don't understand,' you say. 'What about all of these law books that you have read. And what about our legal rights which are set forth in those books. Aren't they important? And shouldn't they be protected?'"

"I'm sorry, but you've got it all wrong again," Mr. Wright, went on. "Those books do not contain your legal rights. They contain your legal penalties. If you are not smart enough, responsible enough, and adult enough to sit down and decide what will happen to your children, then the price that you will pay is that lawyers like me, who are total strangers to your lives, and who have never even met your children, will come in, pull down all of these books from their shelves, and decide what will happen to them. And we will do the same thing when it comes to your money."

CHAPTER 3

Following A Script

When Mark and Susan decided to divorce, why was their first thought to turn to a lawyer? If you are like most divorcing husbands and wives, it may have been your first thought as well.

Needless to say, it is not something you would ever have thought to do in the past when you were faced with decisions that you had to make or problems that you had to solve—run off and turn your lives over to total strangers. In fact, you would have considered that to be a very unnatural thing to do, which is why you never did it.

That necessarily raises a question. If turning to lawyers was not something that you would ever have thought to do in the past, why is it the first thing that you think of doing now? More to the point, where did that thought come from? It came from the script that you are following. To be sure, you are not aware that you are following a script. But you are. We do that all of the time. We don't do that just with little things. We do it when it comes to some of the most important things in our lives as well. In most instances that makes a lot of sense. After all, it would pose no end of problems if we were always required to make up our own script. It would be like having to reinvent the wheel. Thankfully, we don't have to do that. It has all been decided for us. As they say, it is "in the air."

That was the case when the two of you decided to get married. You were given a script and you dutifully followed it. You didn't even have to question your decision to marry. The script did that for you. It told you that if you had those feelings, you would know it was right. And you believed it.

But it went further. It attended to all the important details. The first thing that it told you was that there had to be a ring. Where did that idea come from? You certainly didn't come up with it on your own. You didn't have to. It was in the script. You did not even have to ask yourself whether the stone should be an emerald, a ruby or a diamond. The script told you that it would be a diamond.

The next thing the script told you was that there had to be a ceremony followed by a reception, so you sat down and made a list of the people you would invite and, eventually, where the reception would take place and what you would serve. The script also mentioned a honeymoon and, at least until recently, it told you that the dress always had to be white. It was that simple. More important, you were programmed to follow it. As we say, that is what people do when they get married. To be sure, the script left the details to you, such as whether you would use a ring that had been in your family or go out and buy a new one. If the latter, it also left to you how much you would spend and whether the stone would be a round one, a square one or some other shape. Nevertheless, the script said that it had to be a diamond rather than an emerald or a ruby, and you never questioned it.

Nor was there very much danger in the fact that you just followed the script you were given rather than sat down and made up your own. To be sure, like most people, you probably spent a bit more money than you had intended or perhaps could even afford, and attending to the details turned out to be more time consuming and created more stress than you had expected. But it was a very exciting experience. More important, everyone had a very good time. So who cared and what difference did it make?

Well, it did make a difference. The script that you were given was somewhat misleading. The fact that the two of you had those feelings, which turned out to be more short lived than you were told, didn't guarantee that it was right as the script led you to believe. How could it be reliable when, as you later found out, there was so much that you didn't know about one another? Nor, as you also found out, was there any correlation between the size and cost of the wedding and the success of the marriage. In fact, one had absolutely nothing to do with the other.

As I said, now that you are planning to divorce, you have been given another script. Unfortunately, it is even more misleading than the one you were given when you got married. It is going to make your divorce even more difficult than it already is. The problem is if you are like most divorcing husbands and wives, you believe your script. In fact, you believe it as devoutly as you do your most cherished beliefs. That is why, if you are not careful, you will make the mistake of blindly following it rather than question it as you should.

The first thing your script will tell you and you will devoutly believe it, is now that you are divorcing, you have a legal problem. If someone had told you that when you were planning to get married—that your decision to marry left you with a legal problem—you would not have understood what they were talking about. To be sure, there were certain legal implications in getting married. But that did not mean that you had a legal problem. Your common sense was enough to tell you that. Nevertheless, that is exactly what your script will tell you when it comes to your divorce.

That is only part of the problem, however. Your script will tell you something else that, since you devoutly believe it, you will not question. Unlike Mark and Susan, you can not go off together and get the answers to your questions from one lawyer. Rather you must each go off to separate lawyers, which is a polite way to say that you must turn to adversarial divorce proceedings.

That is what you are unwittingly committing yourself to when you blindly follow that script. Thus, even if you were not aware that you were following a script when you got married, and therefore didn't take the time to carefully examine it, it is critical that you do that now. If you are not careful, it is going to make a mess of your divorce.

To begin with, following that script is going to take a lot longer than you expect. It is also going to cost far more than you can afford. Nor is anyone going to have a good time. Rather, as anyone who has made the mistake of following that script will tell you, it is going to be one of the worst experiences in your life. Needless to say, that is not what you want. Nor can you afford it.

To be sure, if you consult with a divorce lawyer that is not how he (or she) will describe it. On the contrary, he will try to persuade you that following that script not only makes a great deal of sense, but is also your only hope. Your cadre of well meaning advisors may tell you the same thing. They are wrong. It doesn't make any sense. It is nothing but legal nonsense, and dangerous nonsense at that. Nor do you need a law school education to understand that. Your common sense will be enough. That is why, rather than running off blindly and following that script, it is critical that you question it—ask yourself what you are doing and why, and just where it is going to take you.

That is what Mark and Susan did when they consulted with Justin Wright. They had questions that they wanted answers to. But they wanted the same answers, not different ones. As their common sense told them, the only way to get the same answers was to go to the same lawyer. Their common sense told them something else as well. Going off to separate lawyers and being given different answers, as their script insisted, would not have solved their problem. It would only have left them with one.

CHAPTER 4

The Three Problems

I want to return to my silly little story that isn't so silly. I want to tell you the end of the story. When Justin Wright had finished warning Mark and Susan of the serious mistake they would be making were they to turn their lives over to total strangers on no better basis than the fact that they had gone to law school, he turned to them and said, "While I told you that I don't think that the two of you have legal problems just because you have decided to divorce, I never said that you do not have important problems. You do, and I want to tell you what I consider to be the three principal ones." With that, he handed them a piece of paper on which was printed the following:

1. How are we each going to be able to continue to be the important influence in our children's lives in the future that we have been in the past, and how are we each going to be able to enjoy being their parents?
2. What is going to happen to the property that is in our joint and individual names, and if we are going to divide it, how are we going to do that?
3. How are we each going to be able to manage financially in the future, and what obligation, if any, should one of us have to the other (and to our children), based on the circumstances of our marriage, to be concerned with how the other is going to be able to do that?

When they had both had an opportunity to read these questions, he continued. "Since I do not know the two of you, it might seem presumptuous of me to suggest that I know what your three principal problems are. But why would yours be different than anyone else's? They aren't. They are the same problems that every husband and wife who is going through a divorce finds themselves faced with, and it is important that you keep that in mind."

"Since I have a license to practice law," he went on, "and since I have spent years learning to think in legalese, to speak in legalese and to write in legalese, I could have expressed those three problems in legalese. For example, when it came to the first, I could have talked about 'sole custody' and 'joint custody', or about 'legal custody' and 'physical custody'. When it came to the second, I could have invoked the terms 'separate property' and 'marital property', or the 'appreciation in the value of separate property' (at least if you lived in states like New York or Pennsylvania, which recognize those distinctions, but not in states like Massachusetts, which do not). As for the third, I could have talked about 'rehabilitative maintenance', 'non-durational maintenance' or 'permanent maintenance', again at least in those states that employ those terms."

"Had I done that," he continued, "would I have expressed those problems more accurately? No. I would argue that those are the most accurate expression of those problems. All that I would have done would have been to express them in a language which (though not in my case) I was more comfortable with, but at your expense. All that I would have done would have been to subtly inflate my importance and just as subtly put you down, since I am the only person in the room who reads, speaks and writes in this mystical language. It seems to me that if we intend to have a conversation amongst the three of us, it better well be in a language that all three of us understand. Otherwise it is going to be a lecture and a monologue."

"Nevertheless, that is exactly what is going to happen if you follow your script and buy into the legal nonsense that insists that, while this was never true before, now that you are divorcing you have a legal problem. You will run off to a lawyer, whom your script has now made the expert in your life. Nor will you and your lawyer engage in a conversation when you get there. Rather, you will sit politely, hat in hand, and listen while he lectures to you. After all, if you have a legal problem and are no longer the expert in your life, what could you possibly contribute to the conversation? And on what basis could you express an opinion when it came to the answers to any of these questions or solutions to any of these problems? After all, where did you go to law school? Only your attorney did, which is why he, rather than you, is now the expert in your life."

"To be sure, your attorney may acknowledge that it was perfectly appropriate for the two of you to have made the important decisions in your lives in the past without first getting his good opinion. But that was in your marriage. This is now your divorce, and all of that has changed. You have unexpectedly wandered into unchartered legal waters. That is why you need a legal navigator. Not having gone to law school, what knowledge or experience do you have that could possibly enable you to navigate through these waters on your own? Absolutely none."

This does not represent legal sense as your script would have you believe. It is nothing but legal nonsense. Nevertheless, divorcing husbands and wives all too often get taken in by it. When they do, like the children who foolishly followed the Pied Piper of Hamelin's siren call, they will pay dearly for their mistake. Needless to say, you don't want that to happen to you.

CHAPTER 5

An Unnatural Thing

My purpose in telling you what I referred to as a silly little story that is not so silly was not to make fun of the law or to suggest that it does not have a place in your divorce. It does have a place, in fact an important one, and we will have to get to that. Rather, it was to remind you of something that the script you are following has caused you to lose sight of.

This is not the first time in your marriage that the two of you were faced with problems that you had to solve and questions that you had to answer. How did you deal with them in the past? You dealt with them based on your good judgment and the personal considerations that were important to you—what I have characterized as your common sense. The one thing that you did not do was turn to lawyers, who after all are total strangers, and allow them to make those decisions for you. As I said, you would have considered that to be a very unnatural thing to do.

Thus, when you got married, the last thing that would have occurred to you to do was to turn to lawyers to decide when you would get married or where, whom you would invite and what you would serve, or where you would go on your honeymoon. Rather, you made those decisions on your own. To be sure, since this was all new to you, you no doubt did some homework. That probably included talking to many people, particularly those who were going to perform the service and cater the reception. But that didn't mean that you allowed them to make those decisions. After all, it was your wedding not theirs.

But that was in your marriage. This is now your divorce. It makes no difference. It is no less unnatural to turn your lives over to total strangers now just because you are changing the direction in your lives—getting divorced rather than getting married. To be sure, you are going to need help now just as you did then. Nevertheless, your common sense is enough to tell you that you should still stick as close to the natural thing as you can. What would be the opposite of that? Turning your lives over to total strangers, in this case lawyers.

If you do that, on what basis will the decisions in your lives be made? Certainly not on the basis of your common sense—your good judgment and the personal considerations that are important to you. After all, you will not be making those decisions. Your lawyers will. Rather, since a lawyer would not be able to make those decisions on any other basis, they will be made based upon the application of legal rules.

As I said, although the script that you are blindly following has caused you to lose sight of this, those are not the rules that you would have ever thought to look to in the past. On the contrary, your common sense was enough to tell you they were very arbitrary rules having little to do with the reality of your lives. That is why you never allowed lawyers to make the important decision in your lives in the past. Again, you would have considered that to be a very unnatural thing to do. It is no less unnatural now just because you have decided to divorce.

Why, then, do divorcing husbands and wives so often not listen to their common sense? As I said, it is because the script that they have been given has blinded them to what their common sense would tell them by elevating the law to a place of sanctity, putting it on a pedestal and placing a halo around it. We are no longer talking about a set of arbitrary legal rules. We are talking about your God given legal rights. In fact, that is one of the principal purposes of that script—to disable you from being able to see the law objectively for what it is, which is just a set of rules that you could turn to if you cannot find better ones.

This, then, is the issue. How and on what basis are the two of you going to solve the three principal problems that your decision to divorce has left you with? While divorcing husbands and wives do not generally give very much thought to this, there are many procedures that you could employ. The most obvious one would be for the two of you to sit down and solve them on the same basis that you did in your marriage. In other words, you could decide them on the basis of what I have referred to as your common sense. In my terms, that would be the natural thing to do. Anything else, such as turning your lives over to total strangers, would be unnatural.

It is critical that you remember this. Lawyers do not know what is best for you. Nor are they necessarily wise. They are just people who went to law school.

Part II

Legal Sense—Legal Nonsense

CHAPTER 6

When Your Common Sense Is Not Enough

The simple message of this book is that though your divorce is obviously different from your marriage—in the terms here, that it has left you with different questions and different problems than you were faced with in your marriage—it is not so different that you should be persuaded to do something that you would never have thought to do before, namely, turn the personal decisions in your lives over to total strangers, in this case lawyers. After all, there is nothing in their training or experience that makes them experts here.

Nor, unfortunately, is there anything in your training or experience. To be sure, you may not need help when it comes to deciding with whom your children will be and when, and even where they will be—whether or not they will continue to live in their present home—though even here you may have a difference of opinion. But how are you going to answer what will invariably be the most important and difficult question with which you will be faced, namely, the payment, if any, that one of you should make to the other, either for his or her support or that of your children? What in your experience could possibly qualify you to answer this question and make that decision? Nothing. And there will be other questions like this one that you will have to answer as well.

But your unfamiliarity with these questions and the fact that the problems in your divorce are different than those in your marriage is not the only reason why you are going to need help. To understand this, let me return to Mark and Susan. While in the past the two of them may have been able to answer the questions and solve the problems in their lives on their own, without doing something as unnatural as turning to total strangers, they will undoubtedly have far more difficultly doing that now.

There are a number of reasons for this. Moreover, they will be instructive in terms of helping you understand why you will not be able to do this completely on your own, as you have in the past, and why you are going to need help. They will also help you better understand why you would turn to the law for help now when you never did that before, and what its appropriate place and function is. In both cases, the most obvious reason is that the circumstances of your marriage and of your divorce are not the same.

While the two of you obviously had differences of opinion in your marriage, the very fact of your marriage tended to empower you to find a way to resolve those differences, or at least to get past them. That was because you were still united in a common desire to maintain your ongoing relationship, and that served to save the day, even if one or both of you were required to make some compromises or sacrifices in the process, as you no doubt did.

Your decision to divorce, however, is not such an empowering decision. On the contrary, it tends to dis-empower you. To begin with, if you are like most couples, it was not a joint decision. Thus, while the two of you may have wanted to go in the same general direction before, that is probably not the case now. You want to go in different directions, one to end the marriage the other to continue it.

There is another factor that also complicates the matter. Although the two of you may have been married to one another, you inevitably come to your divorce with very different histories of your marriage. Those different histories, and particularly your very different understandings of how and why the two of you have gotten to where you are, are going to dramatically color what you will each feel is appropriate and inappropriate. Nor is there very much that anyone is going to be able to do about that. In fact, if they could get the two of you to agree on the history of your marriage, they might be able to save your marriage. But they are not going to be able to do that.

But there is more to it than that. Divorcing husbands and wives invariably feel that they are where they are because of what the other has done or been unwilling to do. As a result, they each tend to see themselves as being the innocent victim in the tragedy that is unfolding in their lives. Put another way, neither is able to see his or her role in what has happened—I didn't say fault, I just said role. And since husbands and wives do not get married to get divorced, and since this is not where they wish to be or feel they deserve to be, they are inevitably overwhelmed by difficult feelings that will invariably interfere with their ability to resolve these questions on their own. In fact were they to attempt to do that, there is always the danger that those feelings might get so out of hand that their discussions will tend to generate more heat than light, and not be very productive. That is why they will need help.

There is something else when it comes to the feelings that husbands and wives experience at the time of their divorce that will add to their problem. Husbands and wives who feel trapped in a marriage that has failed to meet their needs and expectations very commonly express their frustration and sense of injustice in ways that only adds fuel to the fire. The conventional wisdom is that the things that they say and do are what caused the problems in their marriage. The truth is that what they say and do are the inevitable consequence of the problems in their marriage. It makes no difference. The party who feels that he or she has been the victim of all of this is going to cite it as proof of the other's being responsible for their divorce and the one at fault.

This will be a problem even if what has been said and done is the garden variety of conduct that unhappily married husbands and wives engage in. It will become far more of a problem, however, when, as is so commonly the case today, one of them has looked outside of the marriage for emotional support. It makes no difference that this outside relationship is just an act of desperation. Nor does it make any difference that, as is the case in the vast majority of instances, it is simply a bridge relationship that will go nowhere. It will do too much emotional damage to the other person's sense of himself or herself for them to see it as anything other than an act of betrayal.

These then are the emotional considerations that will make solving the problems in your divorce different and more difficult than was the case when it came to solving the problems in your marriage. But there are certain practical considerations that will make it more difficult as well. The first, of course, is that the problems you are faced with now are very different than the problems you were faced with in the past. During your marriage, you were never required to ask yourselves how much would be appropriate for you to spend to support your children. In fact, you would have considered that to be a rather meaningless question. It is not meaningless now, however. On the contrary, one of the questions that you will have to answer is just how much one of you will be required to pay to the other for that purpose. You will also have to ask another question, namely, whether it would be appropriate for one of you to make a payment to the other for his or her support and, if so, how much and for how long. What in your previous experience could possibly qualify you to answer these questions and make these decisions? Unfortunately, nothing.

This brings me to the second practical problem. I call it the problem of the table and the tablecloth. The table represents your problem. The tablecloth represents the resources that you have to cover your problem. The tablecloth used to be large enough, or barely large enough, to cover the table. But the problem has now gotten bigger. While there was only one household to support in the past, now there will be two. While there used to be only one electric bill to pay at the beginning of the month, now there will be a second. And so it will go, right down the line. Unfortunately, in most instances at least, while your table (your problem) will have increased in size, your tablecloth (your resources) will stay the same. The tablecloth is going to be too small for the table.

The third practical problem is a little different. In the past, you were only required to take one day at a time. Thus, when you got up in the morning, you were only required to decide what you were going to have for dinner that day, and very few of us would have difficulty doing that. But if I asked you what you were going to have for dinner the next 365 days, you would not know where to start. We just don't think that way. As I said, it is one day at a time.

Unfortunately, that is how you are going to have to think now. Husbands and wives going through their divorce feel that they are being asked to put their whole lives on the table and decide everything at once. Needless to say, that can be a little overwhelming. How do you deal with the future when you don't know what the future will look like?

This is why you are going to need help now even if you didn't need it in the past. To use a metaphor that I often employ, husbands and wives faced with the prospect of their divorce commonly feel as if they are faced with an immense forest that they have to get through and over the mountain to the clearing on the other side, and no one wants to have to go through a forest alone, particularly at night. It would be nice to have the hand of someone who has been through this territory and is familiar with it.

This is why you are going to need help. Not because you have a legal problem, as your script would have you believe. Rather, because the emotional and practical problems that you will find yourselves faced with are going to make it far more difficult for the two of you to do in your divorce what you were able to do in your marriage. To be sure, your common sense will still go a long way in helping you solve these problems and answer these questions. But it will only take you so far.

CHAPTER 7

Legal Rules—Legal Rights

You are going to need help. We have established that. The question is what kind of help do you need and from whom are you going to get it? Before I address this, it is necessary to make one preliminary observation.

In referring to the law, I have repeatedly talked in terms of legal rules. In fact, I have suggested that the law represents a very arbitrary set of legal rules having little if anything to do with the reality of your lives. That is not how your script refers to the law, however. Rather, it always characterizes the law, and refers to it, as representing your *legal rights*.

That is certainly a far more flattering description than mine. After all, it is hard to get too worked up about legal rules. They are cold and impersonal. They have nothing to do with us. Legal rights, on the other hand, are very different. They are personal to us. We also consider them to be very important, which is why that characterization has so much more appeal. Thus, while I would not get very far trying to persuade you that it is important for you to protect your legal rules, I will have no difficulty when it comes to your legal rights. There is no sacrifice that would be too great to ask when it comes to them.

That is why your script describes the law in the lofty terms that it does. It is trying to persuade you to do something very unnatural, which is to turn your lives over to total strangers, in this case lawyers, and to the legal rules that they employ. Better to sanctify the law, put it on a pedestal, and place a halo around it. Better not to point out what your common sense would be enough to tell you, namely, that one person's legal right is another person's legal penalty. After all, if one of you has a legal right to get something, then the other's legal penalty is that he or she will have to give it to you. Characterizing all of this in terms of legal rights may get you not to see this. But it doesn't change anything. As they say, there are no free lunches.

The question isn't whether my characterization is flattering or unflattering to the law. It is whether it is accurate. In fact, that is the critical question. The two of you are going to have to look to the law for answers to your questions. As I said, for better or worse, your common sense will not be enough. But if you are looking to the law then, rather than just following it blindly wherever it leads, it is appropriate to ask yourself just where it is going to take you. In other words, just how good an instrument are the legal rules that the law employs? Will they leave you with the right answers to your questions? Will they leave you any answers? Or are they just going to leave you with a long philosophical debate, going nowhere, as to what those answers should be?

Your common sense is enough to tell you that those are the questions you should be asking before you turn your life over to those rules. Nevertheless, characterizing the law in terms of legal rights, as your script does, has the effect of muting those questions. We do not ask questions of sacred objects, let alone judge them. We place them on a pedestal and worship them. That is what your script would have you do when it comes to the law.

But what of your legal rights? Are they of no consequence? They are, which is why I want you to know them. You have two legal rights. The two of you can sit down as responsible adults and attempt to answer your questions and solve your problems with a view to concluding an agreement that both of you feel you can live with. Or you can go off, follow your script, and make a game of it, the object of which is simply to get as much as you can and to give as little as you have to, your husband or wife be damned. Those are your legal rights, and all the rest is just talk. It is critical that you remember this.

CHAPTER 8

Getting Help

When it comes to getting help, there are three questions that are important for you to ask and answer. The first, which we have already answered, is why you will need help. As we have seen, that is because the two of you are not going to be able to answer all of the questions and solve all of the problems that you now find yourselves faced with on your own as you have in the past. The second is, what kind of help do you need? The third is, how are you going to get that help?

Before I address these three questions, however, I want to go back to the distinction that I made between problems that the two of you will have to solve and questions that you will have to answer. By problems, I am referring to those issues which do not require any special knowledge let alone expert opinion, such as with whom your children will be and when, and even where they will be. Your common sense should be all that you need here. Thus, if you have a problem here, it will just be in the fact that you may have a difference of opinion when it comes to this.

The questions that you will have to answer, such as what payment will be made by one of you to the other either for his or her support of for the support of your children, are a little different. To be sure, your previous experience and your common sense may be of some help. Nevertheless, they are not likely to be sufficient when it comes to these. As I said, these are just not the kinds of questions that you were faced with in the past. Thus, if you are looking for help here, it is not necessarily because you have a difference of opinion. In many instances you will not have any opinion, at least any opinion worth anything. It is because you need an answer. And if you are looking to lawyers and the law for that purpose, it is simply because there is no other place to look.

I will have to return to the help you will need to resolve whatever differences of opinion you may have. When it comes to these, you are going to look for a different kind of help, and to a different place to get it, than will be the case with the questions that you will have to answer. The law is not going to be of much help when it comes to those differences of opinion. It will be no better able to resolve them than Alexander the Great was able to unravel the Gordian Knot. The law's solution will therefore be very much the same as Alexander's, which will be simply to end the matter (cut through it) by deciding the case.

In the discussion that follows, therefore, I am going to limit myself to the questions that you will have to answer rather than the problems that you will have to solve and the differences of opinion that they may generate. As I said, I will return to the help you will need when it comes to those differences of opinion at a later point. With that in mind, I want to return to the three questions that I said that you had to ask and answer when it came to getting help.

The script that you are following would lead you to believe that there is only one question here. It does this by characterizing the questions that you are faced with as being legal questions—in my terms, as being a legal problem. Nevertheless, your common sense is enough to tell you that there are three questions, not one. Thus, even if you have a legal problem, and therefore need legal answers to your questions, as your script would have you believe, that only answers the first two questions. It doesn't answer the third, namely, how are you going to get those answers. To be sure, your script would have you believe that you only have one choice here. You must each go off to separate lawyers to get those answers. You don't need more than your common sense to tell you that that is not your only choice.

Let us consider this. There is nothing in the fact that you have a legal problem that dictates that you have to go off to separate lawyers to get those answers. That is certainly not what you did in your marriage when you were faced with personal problems that had legal implications. Not even a divorce lawyer would have suggested that. However, the script that you have been given doesn't want you to see this. It would give away the game. That is why it conflates the three questions. It does that in two ways. First, by characterizing your problem as being, not a personal problem that simply has certain legal implications, but as a legal problem. Second, by invoking the cornerstone on which our adversarial legal system is grounded, namely, that the two of you have conflicting interests. It is those conflicting interests, supposedly, that militate that you must get those answers from separate lawyers. At least that is what your script would have you believe.

I want to put aside for the moment the question of how you are going to get the help that you need—get the answers to your questions, and whether what a divorce lawyer characterizes as your conflicting interests really requires you to go off to separate lawyers to get those answers. I will address that at a later point. Rather, I want to address the second question, namely, what kind of help do you need. I am going to suggest that this question necessarily gives rise to another. Again, it a question that your script does not want you to see, even though it is the most important one. That question is, what does it mean to be of help?

I have argued that you need help because your common sense alone is not going to be sufficient now, as it was in the past, to answer all of your questions. I have also suggested that if you turn to the law for answers to those questions, it is not because you have a legal problem, as divorce lawyers would have you believe. It is, first, because you feel that the law will be able to provide you with answers to those questions and, second, and more important, because you do not know where else to turn. If there were some other place you could turn to, you would not have to look to the law. In other words, contrary to what your script would have you believe, the law is only second best, which is why you would never have thought to turn to it in the past. It is a court of last resort when all else fails. Ironically, despite all of a divorce lawyer's fanfare about your legal rights, even he will tell you this. No one wants to go to court.

I suggested that the question, what kind of help do you need?, necessarily gives rise to another, namely, what does it mean to be of help? I now want to rehearse what would satisfy that second question. I am going to suggest that in terms of the questions that you will be faced with in your divorce, any procedure to which you turn to for answers to your questions should fulfill the following five requirements.

1. It should leave you with an answer, not just a debate going nowhere, as to what that answer is.
2. It shouldn't leave you with just any answer. It should leave you with the right answer.

3. It shouldn't cost a king's ransom to get that answer.
4. It shouldn't take forever and a day to get it.
5. Finally, getting that answer should not exact an emotional price that will only make it more difficult for you to bring closure to the difficult feelings that are the inevitable by-product of your divorce.

Needless to say, you do not need a law school education to understand that you would expect any procedure that you turn to for help to satisfy these five requirements. Again, your common sense will be enough to tell you this. Nevertheless, you will not find any mention of them in your script. It is as if none of these requirements count for anything. There is a reason for this. Were your script to underscore these necessary requirements, that would only cause you to look at that script, and to question it, more carefully than you have. Worse, you might come to the realization that it does not satisfy even one of those requirements. In short, it might cause you to decide not to follow it. From the standpoint of a divorce lawyer, that will obviously not do.

How does your script get you to blindly learn your lines and play the part that has been assigned to you? I have suggested that it does this by conflating the three questions that you necessarily have to ask and answer when it comes to how you are going to get help. It conflates them by characterizing the undertaking in terms of lofty abstractions. That is always what we do when we give people a script that sends them off to do mindless battle. Thus, just as we talk about *freedom* and *democracy* when we send our young men and women off to do battle in foreign lands, only to come back bloodied, bruised, and sometimes not at all, so too that is what we do when we send divorcing husbands and wives off to do battle with one another. Invoking lofty abstractions, we talk about their *legal rights* and tell them that the object of their endeavor is to secure an agreement that is *fair* and *equitable*. Worse, they are so taken in by those abstractions that it puts to sleep their critical faculties. As a result, they do not see what they are not supposed to see, which is that the script that they have been given will not satisfy even one of these five necessary requirements. But that, of course, is the intended effect of those abstractions.

CHAPTER 9

Taking Forever and Costing
a Small Fortune

I said that there are five requirements that any procedure you employ should satisfy. Two of those are that it should leave you with an answer and that the answer it leaves you with should be the right one. Before I turn to those two requirements, however, I need to address the other three. However, since the procedure outlined in your script so clearly violates each and every one, it will not be necessary to spend very much time on them.

With that in mind, I want to assume that your script could guarantee that you will be left with an answer to your question and that the answer will be the right one. Wouldn't that be the end of it? Would there be anything else that had to be said? To be sure, that is what your script would have you believe. That is why it characterizes the procedure it insists you must follow in terms of your *legal rights* and what is *fair* and *equitable.* It wants to disable you from being able to see what you are not supposed to see, namely, that that is not the end of it. Nor will it be difficult to prove.

Suppose I were to tell you that, just as your script says, the application of legal rules is guaranteed to leave you with an agreement that protects your legal rights and is fair and equitable. Suppose I were to go further and say that as evidence of that, I will give you my bond, in any amount you ask, to assure it. However, unlike the authors of that script, because I believe in what we refer to as truth in lending, just as you are about to sign on the dotted line I say, "But I need to tell you something before you do. Everything that I have told you is absolutely true. If you follow the script that you have been given, you will be left with exactly what I said. But since everything has a price, I want you to know what that price is before you make your decision. To be sure, the procedure you will be following is a wonderful one. Nevertheless, it is going to take forever, cost a small fortune, and exact a terrible emotional price, not only on you, but on your children as well."

To be sure, you will be left with the right answers to your questions—what divorce lawyers characterize as an agreement that will protect your legal rights and be fair and equitable. But will that now be enough? Put another way, is the cost irrelevant? To be sure, your script does not talk about that cost. It does not want you to see it. If you did, you might have second thoughts about blindly following it. You might even decide to throw it in the garbage can, which is what your common sense would tell you to do.

Again, that is the effect of all of the lofty abstractions that divorce lawyers forever invoke to sell their wares. They blind us to the cost. After all, we do not question the cost when what is at issue is *freedom* and *our way of life*. On the contrary, those are the kinds of things that we have been brought up to lay down our lives for if it comes to that. Similarly, we do not question the cost when what is at issue are our *legal rights* and what is *fair* and *equitable*. When it comes to those, no price can be too great. At least that is what your script would have you believe.

To be sure, that may be true if what is at issue is what we characterize as our inalienable rights—our right of free speech, to practice the religion of our choice, etc. It is quite another thing, however, if all that is at issue is a set of arbitrary legal rules. After all, we have had different rules in the past. We will undoubtedly have different rules in the future. These are just the rules that we happen to have today, and all of the lofty abstraction in the world will not change that. They just disable us from being able to see it.

I am not going to waste your time documenting that the procedure that your script would have you follow is guilty of all of those sins. I don't have to. There is nothing that I could tell you that someone who has made the mistake of following that script has not already told you better than I could. As we say, everyone knows it.

CHAPTER 10

The Problem and the Procedure

I said that the script you are following is going to get you into a lot of trouble. I have already indicated one of the ways in which it will do that. It is going to send you off on a wild goose chase that will take forever and cost a small fortune. As if that is not enough, it is going to exact a terrible emotional price as well. Nevertheless, your script has led you to believe that you will at least be left with the right answer for your pains. You won't be. In fact, though your script has not told you this, you are not going to be left with any answer at all. I appreciate that this will seem somewhat incredible. But, as you will shortly see, it isn't.

Before I get to that, however, I want to indicate two other ways that your script is going to get you into trouble. The first will be to cause you to confuse your problem with the procedure that you will employ to solve it. The second is that you will become so engrossed in that procedure that you will completely lose sight of your problem.

Let us consider the first of these. Mark and Susan cannot agree who will keep their grandfather clock. As I will characterize it, they have a difference of opinion here. Mark feels that he should keep it because it was a gift to him from Susan's father and because it has always been in his study. Susan feels that she should keep it because it belonged to her grandfather and has been in her family for generations. She also argues that her father would never have given the clock to Mark had Mark not been married to her and that he certainly would not have given it to Mark had he known that the two of them would be divorcing. How are they going to decide this? In the terms here, if they are unable to do so on any other basis, what procedure are they going to employ to resolve their problem here?

I suggest a solution. I tell them that I have a procedure that they could employ. It is very inexpensive, it will only take them a few seconds, and it is sure to solve their problem. To add weight to my recommendation, I tell them that it is probably the finest problem solving procedure that has ever been devised. They even use it at the beginning of every Super Bowl game to decide which team will have the right to receive or kick off. With that I take a quarter out of my pocket and place it between my thumb and index finger. "Watch," I say. And with that I flip it into the air with my right hand, catch it, and then turn it over onto the back of my left hand, keeping it covered with my right hand. "Heads, you win," I say to one of them, "tails you win," I say to the other. "It is that simple." With that I have each of them practice flipping the coin. When they have each done that a few times, I say, "You see, what the two of you have is a coin flipping problem."

At that point one of them jumps in and abruptly stops me. "We don't have a coin flipping problem. Our problem is that we have a difference of opinion when it comes to which one of us will have the right to keep the grandfather clock. This coin is just the procedure that you have recommended that we employ to solve that problem. Let's not confuse the two. Besides, we are not very happy with the procedure that you have recommended. This grandfather clock may not seem very important to you, but it is to us, which is why neither of us feels very comfortable leaving the question of who will have the right to keep it to chance, which, when all is said and done, is what we will be doing if we employ your coin."

"There is something else about the procedure you recommended that we are not very happy with. We noticed it when we were practicing flipping your coin. After but a short time, we found that we became so engrossed in flipping the coin we completely lost sight of the problem that your coin was supposed to solve, namely our grandfather clock. I am sorry, but you are going to have to come up with a better procedure than that."

"All right," I reply. "You are not happy with the procedure that I have recommended. You want a better one. That is fine. But before I suggest another one, I want to remind you of something. If you are going to employ some other procedure, it ought to have all of the virtues of the one

I recommended and then some. Otherwise you would be better off using my coin. Thus, when you consider another procedure, you must keep something in mind. You may not have been happy with my lowly coin. But it did meet four of your five requirements. It was quick; it only took a few seconds. It was anything but expensive; it only cost twenty-five cents. Getting an answer didn't cause any emotional wear and tear. In fact, there were no emotions involved at all. Finally, it not only provided you with an answer, the answer was also clear. It was either heads or tails. In fact, you only have one complaint. It didn't leave you with the right answer."

This brings us to the critical question. Will the two of you be left with the right answer if you employ the procedure outlined in your script? Just as important, will you be left with any answer? Though you do not know this, and though no one has told you, the answer is no on both counts. You will not be left with the right answer. Worse, you will not be left with any answer, at least any answer that will be of help to you.

Before I get to that, however, I want to return to what I said at the beginning of this discussion, namely, that the script you have been given is going to cause you to confuse your problems with the procedure that you have been told to employ to solve them, and that within no time at all you will become so engrossed in that procedure that you will completely lose sight of the problems that you turned to it to solve.

This is where all of the lofty abstractions that divorce lawyers forever invoke come into play. The problem, as we all agreed, is your grandfather clock and who is going to keep it. If you are being encouraged to turn to the application of legal rules to resolve it, like my lowly coin, those legal rules are not your problem. In other words, you do not have a legal rules problem or, as a divorce lawyer likes to say, a legal problem, any more than you would have had a coin problem had you decided to employ a coin to resolve it. Your problem is your grandfather clock. Thus, like the quarter I recommended, the application of legal rules is just the procedure that you will employ if you follow your script. As such, it must be judged by the same test that we employed in considering my lowly coin. It must satisfy the same five requirements that we agreed any procedure you employed should meet.

For a divorce lawyer, that will not do. As we have seen, the procedure he recommends has already failed three of those five requirements, and not by just a little bit, but by a mile. As we will see shortly, it is going to fail the other two requirements as well. Thus, it will not do for you to put that procedure to the same test that you put my coin. If you do, my coin is going to look much better than it does now. In fact, you will begin to understand why I said that it is the finest problem solving procedure that has ever been devised. Thus, better for a divorce lawyer to get your eye off the mark. Better if you do not put the procedure that he is going to recommend to the test.

How do divorce lawyers accomplish this? Again, that is where all of the lofty abstractions come in. First, they do not refer to the law as representing simply a set of arbitrary legal rules which, as you will see, is all that they really are. That would only be to give away the game. They get your eye off the mark by elevating their importance. Thus, they refer to them, not as legal rules, but as your *legal rights*. The effect of this is to cause you to put these legal rules on a par with what you consider to be your inalienable rights, like your right to marry whom you choose. The effect of this, as I said, is to conflate the three problems that you started out with and make it seem as if you have just one, namely, to secure your legal rights.

Unfortunately, characterizing everything in terms of lofty abstractions has a very unfortunate effect. It will cause you to lose sight of your problem. That was never really a danger when it came to my lowly coin. It never caused you to lose sight of the grandfather clock, except perhaps for a minute. Nor did it so blind you that you failed to ask the relevant question, namely, just how effective a procedure is it? In other words, the coin never became an end in itself. It always remained what it was, just a means to an end—a procedure.

But these abstractions will have another unfortunate effect as well. They will cause you to lose sight of the cost involved in turning to the procedure that you are being encouraged to employ—in my terms, the cost of getting answers to your questions. To be sure, the grandfather clock is important. It even has a sentimental value that it is not possible to quantify in dollars and cents. But unlike "freedom" and "democracy" or, in this case, your "legal rights," its value is not without limit. It is not something that you would lay down your life for. That being the case, the cost involved in getting those answers, not only the cost in terms of time and money but also the considerable emotional cost, is not only relevant but critical.

It is critical for another reason as well. Divorcing husbands and wives who follow that script do so because they believe that their reward will be to be left with an agreement that is fair and equitable. That, at least, is what they believed when they started out. However, it is not how they will feel by the time it ends. Even though they paid the terrible price it required, neither of them will feel that is what they got. Rather, they will feel that what they were left with represents nothing but an injustice. The necessary effect of this will be to leave them more hurt and more angry when they get through than they were when they began. That is the sad legacy bequeathed to those who make the mistake of following that script. The irony is that everyone knows this.

CHAPTER 11

Will the Application of Legal Rules Leave You with the Right Answer?

This brings us back to the five requirements that we said any procedure you turn to should satisfy. As we have already found, the procedure that your script recommends will fail three of those requirements, and not just by a little bit but by a mile. The question is whether it will at least satisfy the last two.

Before we address that, however, it is necessary to rehearse again why we are looking to the law in the first place. It is because, if what I have called your common sense is not going to be enough, the only other place that you can turn to is the law. That is because it is only the law that has expressed an opinion when it comes to these questions. For example, every state has what it refers to as child support guidelines that are employed by the court to make a decision with respect to the payment that is to be made by one parent to the other for the support of their children. Thus, if you cannot decide what the appropriate payment should be based on your common sense, or cannot decide that completely on that basis, you will have no choice but to turn to the law.

That is all well and good. Unfortunately, your script is very misleading when it comes to the law or, as I would characterize it, the legal rules that the law provides. That is why blindly following that script is going to get you into trouble. It does not portray those legal rules as something that you can turn to when your common sense is not enough—in my terms, as an aid to your common sense. It portrays them as something that you should substitute for your common sense.

How does your script justify this? We have already seen one of the ways, namely, by characterizing the problem that you find yourself confronted with as being a legal problem and the purpose of the undertaking that you are about to embark on as being that of securing your legal rights. It does it in another way as well. It insists that it is not possible for you to make informed, intelligent decisions with respect to the questions that you will have to answer except by turning to, and basing those decision on, the legal rules that the law employs.

Contrary to what your script may tell you, this does not represent legal sense. It is nothing but legal nonsense, and it is important that you remember this. Legal rules are arbitrary rules having little if anything to do with the realities of your lives, which is one of the reasons why it would never have occurred to you to look to them in the past. They are only important if your common sense is not enough. As such, legal rules never trump your common sense. Your common sense always trumps legal rules.

One example will be sufficient. Several years ago, your eldest child was about to graduate from high school and enter college. The question that you were faced with was the payment of his (or her) college education expenses, and the two of you sat down to discuss this.

On what basis did you make that decision? On the basis of your good judgment and the personal considerations that were important to you—what I have characterized as your common sense. Those personal considerations necessarily included how important it was to you that your son have the benefit of a college education, what it would cost and how much you could afford.

Did those personal considerations also include the law—in my terms, the answer that you would have gotten had you looked to the application of legal rules to get it? After all, the script that you have been given says that it is important that you make informed, intelligent decisions, and it does not credit your common sense as being sufficient for that purpose. Rather, it insists that, to do so, you must know what your legal rights and obligations are. Does that make sense—in my terms, does that represent legal sense? Or is it just legal nonsense?

Let us consider this. If the two of you live in the state of New York, you would not have been obligated to support your son in college beyond the first semester of his junior year. He turned 21 at that time, and a parent in New York does not have an obligation to support a child beyond the age of 21. If you lived in Florida or California, you would not have had any obligation to support him in college at all, since a parent's obligation to support a child in those states ends when a child turns 18, which your son did just before he was about to enter college.

Was it possible for the two of you to make a decision here without knowing any of this? Of course it was. The proof of this is the fact that married husbands and wives do that all of the time. On what basis do they make their decisions? As I said, on the basis of what I have characterized as their common sense.

That raises the necessary question. Would the two of you have had second thoughts about this if a friend of yours, who happened to be a lawyer, told you that, based on the law in your state, you didn't have any legal obligation to pay for your son's college education expenses? The question is a rhetorical one. You would not have known what he was talking about let alone why he was telling you this. After all, most of the things that you had done for your children that you were most proud of were things that you knew you didn't have any legal obligation to do. Who cared and what difference did it make?

As you will find, it will make a very big difference now if you make the mistake of following the script that you have been given. That script will insist that it is not only important but critical that you know what answers the application of legal rules will leave you with before you make any of the important decisions in your divorce—in the terms here, know whether you have a legal obligation to do something before you undertake it. In other words, it will persuade you that what may have been perfectly appropriate in your marriage is not appropriate in your divorce. Worse, you will be so taken in by your script that you will believe this. It makes no difference that you would have dismissed this suggestion as being nothing more than legal nonsense at any other time in your lives. You won't now. That is what I meant when I said earlier that you will believe your script as devoutly as you do your most cherished beliefs.

But that script will do something more. It will subtly discourage you from asking the questions of the procedure it recommends that I have suggested are critical. Again, that is where all of the lofty abstractions will come in. When it comes to the things that we elevate, place on a pedestal and put a halo around, we don't question them, let alone insist that they pass any test. To be sure, that may be true of common currency, like the arbitrary legal rules that the law employs. It is not true, however, when it comes to those things that we have sanctified, like your legal rights.

Nevertheless, despite all of the lofty abstractions that your script invokes when it comes to the law, that is all that it is, just an arbitrary set of legal rules having little to do with the realities of your lives. Thus, before you leave the important decisions in your lives to them, it is important that you ask whether their application will meet the other two tests that we said any procedure you employ should satisfy. After all, if those rules are no more guaranteed to leave you with the right answer in your divorce than they were in your marriage, why would you make your decisions based on them. In the terms that I have put it, why would you allow legal rules to trump your common sense? If you had any sense, you wouldn't.

With that in mind, let us take one of those situations in which your common sense may be sufficient to take you part of the way, but not the whole way. I referred to it before. That is when it comes to the payment that one of you should make to the other either for his or her support or for that of your children. How are you going to decide how much that payment should be and, if it is for the support of the other, how long that payment should be made? Again, what in your previous experience would qualify you to answer those questions? Nothing. That is why your common sense may not be enough.

If you are looking to the law for the answers here it is not just because you do not have anywhere else to turn. It is because you have been led to believe that the law will not only give you answers to your questions but, more important, that they will be the right answers.

Unfortunately, your script has not told you the whole story. To be more accurate, it has not told it to you straight. The application of legal rules will not leave you with the right answers to your questions. Turning to them will not even leave you with an answer, or at least a clear one. All that you will be left with is a debate, going nowhere, as to what those answers should be. It is critical that you understand this.

With that in mind, I now want to return to the second of what I argued are the five necessary requirements of any procedure that you would employ to get help, in this case to get answers to your questions, namely, that the answers you will be given will be the right ones. Certainly that does not seem to be a very hard requirement to satisfy. Isn't that what securing your legal rights means—to be left with the right answers to your questions? And isn't that what the application of legal rules is guaranteed to do? That is certainly what your script has told you. I also know that you believe it. Nevertheless, there is absolutely no basis for it. In fact, it is nothing but legal nonsense. Moreover, it will not be very hard to demonstrate.

For that purpose, let us compare the rules that lawyers employ with another set of rules, those employed by mathematicians. In both cases they are applied to answer a question. In both cases we have every confidence that they will not only leave us with an answer, but that the answer we will be given will be the right one. That is why you turn to mathematicians when you have a mathematical problem. It is the same reason, so your script tells you, you should turn to lawyers if you have a legal problem.

Suppose I were to tell you that mathematicians in the various states do not employ the same rules. Rather, the rules that they employ differ from state to state. Certainly, that would tend to undermine your faith in the application of those rules. After all, one of the reasons why you have so much faith in the rules of mathematics is that they are universal—they are the same everywhere.

Nevertheless, that is exactly the case when it comes to legal rules. They vary from state to state. Moreover, those differences are not just with respect to little things. They are with respect to some of the most basic things—for example, whether the court has the power to give one of you an interest in property owned by the other at the time of your marriage or acquired by the other by gift or inheritance during your marriage. In some states it does. In others it doesn't. The point is that while every lawyer in a particular state may believe with all his heart and soul that the only way to conclude an agreement that is fair and equitable is to look to the legal rules that are applied in his state, nevertheless, in the state adjoining his, or in a state one or two removed, very different legal rules are applied. Moreover, every lawyer in those other states will attach the same complementary label "fair and equitable" to the answers that the application of the rules in their state will leave you with.

But it is worse than that. Suppose I were to go further and tell you that, even in the same state, where all mathematicians apply the exact same rules, no two mathematicians will ever give you the same answer—ever agree on what the right answer is. What little faith you might still have in the application of mathematical rules would now have been completely undermined. How could the application of mathematical rules possibly leave you with the right answer if no two mathematicians ever applied them in the same way or, therefore, came up with the same answer.

Nevertheless, that is exactly the case when it comes to the application of legal rules. There are no two lawyers that the two of you could go to who will give you the same answer. Worse, their answers will not be just a little different. They will be miles apart. Ironically, divorcing husbands and wives know this. Nevertheless, they still run off to separate lawyers to get those answers.

There is one last thing that has to be said about legal rules and the difference between those rules and the rules of mathematics. A mathematician does not talk about your mathematical rights. Nor does he say that the application of mathematical rules will leave you with an answer that is fair and equitable. Rather, he says that it will leave you with the right answer.

Why do mathematicians not use the same window dressing that divorce lawyers do to sell their wares? They don't have to. You know that mathematics is an exact science and that the application of mathematical rules will leave you with the one and only one right answer. That is why, if you had a mathematical problem, you would go off together to one mathematician rather than employ two. What would be the point in that? It would only increase the cost. To be sure, one of you might hope the answer will be 10 and the other 6. But that does not change the answer.

It does change the answer, however, when, following your script, the two of you go off to separate lawyers. You assume that, like mathematicians, the legal rules that your respective lawyers will employ represent a strict procedure. You also assume that this is what the lawyer with whom you consult will be doing, namely, following that procedure, which is why you will accept the answer that he gives to you as being gospel.

You will be wrong on both counts. Unlike mathematics, the application of legal rules does not represent a strict procedure. Rather, it is a game. More important, divorce lawyers do not apply those rules to get you the right answer. They play the game to get you the best answer.

Ironically, divorcing husbands and wives know this. Nevertheless, they turn to divorce lawyers and to the legal rules that they employ anyway, which shows just how powerful the script they are following is. Worse they do this in a way that is only guaranteed to leave them with different answers to the same question. They go off to separate lawyers.

CHAPTER 12

Playing a Game, Following a Procedure

Needless to say, you do not want to make a game out of your divorce. It is too serious for that. There is also too great a price to be paid. Rather, you want to make as much sense out of it as you can. That will be difficult enough as it is. That is because it is going to require you to try to make sense out of something that, on a fundamental level, doesn't make any sense at all. You do not want to add to your burden by making a game out of it.

Nevertheless, that is exactly what you will be doing if you follow your script. You will be playing a game, in this case a game of legal chess. To be sure, that is not how your script has characterized it. Divorce lawyers would not sell too many of their scripts if it characterized the undertaking in those terms. Rather, it would have you believe that what you will be committing yourself to is a rational procedure, not a game. As I will demonstrate, it is anything but that. It is a game pure and simple.

With that in mind, let us consider how we would characterize the rules that are employed in a fixed procedure, such as mathematics, and those that are employed in a game, such as a game of chess.

1. The basic characteristics of a strict procedure:
    a. A strict procedure follows fixed rules.
    b. A strict procedure excludes all moves but one.
    c. A strict procedure excludes discretion.
    d. A strict procedure excludes strategy.
    e. A strict procedure excludes chance.

     f.   A strict procedure does not tell you in advance where you are going to end up.

     g.   You do not judge the outcome of a strict procedure.

2. The basic characteristics of a game:
   a.   A game follows rules.
   b.   A game permits all moves except excluded moves.
   c.   A game includes discretion.
   d.   A game includes strategy.
   e.   A game includes chance.
   f.   A game tells you in advance where you should end up.
   g.   You do judge the outcome of a game.

All that it is necessary to do is outline these characteristics to tell you what you will be committing yourself to if you follow your script. As I said, it is a game pure and simple. It would be polite to call it a game of legal chess. It would be more accurate to call it what it is, a legal tug-of-war, the object of which is simply to come away with as much as you can get and to give away as little as you have to. And as is the case in all tugs-of-war, someone always gets dragged through the mud.

To be sure, your script does not present it that way. It would have you believe that following it represents a rational procedure. Nevertheless, the last characteristic of a game gives it away. While you do not judge the outcome of a fixed procedure, you do judge the outcome of a game. As we say, someone is a winner and someone is a loser.

That, of course, is how a lawyer judges the outcome of the undertaking outlined in your script. As he says, when litigants go to court, someone wins and someone loses. The irony is that, as everyone knows and as anyone will tell you, when husbands and wifes go to court, no one wins.

But I am getting ahead of myself. Before I get to that, it is necessary to turn to the last requirement that we have agreed any procedure that you turn to should satisfy. As we have already seen, the procedure outlined in the script that you have been given will not leave you with the right answer. Will it at least leave you with an answer? I now want to turn to that. Before I do, however, it is necessary to turn to one last thing.

CHAPTER 13

Legal Sense—Legal Nonsense

Your object is to conclude an agreement. That is because concluding an agreement is the precondition to your being able to effectuate a separation and divorce and to go on with the business of your lives. In order to do that, however, there are certain questions that you must answer and problems that you must solve.

As we have seen, you are not going to be able to do this now as easily or on the same basis as you did in the past. As I put it, in certain instances your common sense may not be enough. To be sure, it will still take you a long way. But it may not take you the whole way. That is why you are going to need help.

I also acknowledged that to get that help, you are going to have to turn to the law—to the legal rules the law in your state applies to answer these questions. Nevertheless, it is important to keep in mind why you are looking to those rules. Divorce lawyers would have you believe that you are looking to them because they will leave you with the right answer—as they characterize it, with an agreement that is fair and equitable. As you have seen, they could not possibly do that, and you must disabuse yourself of that idea. Thus, if you look to them it is because, more modestly, you are looking for an answer and you do not have anywhere else to look.

If the application of legal rules will provide you with an answer, the law will have been of great help to you. It makes no difference that because legal rules differ from state to state, the answer that their application will provide could not possibly be the right one. If the two of you are willing to accept it, the law will have served its purpose, which was to help the two of you conclude an agreement. When it does that, the law deserves to be complimented. That is what I mean when I refer to it as representing legal sense.

As you will see, whether the application of legal rules will or will not serve that purpose will depend upon how you get information about the law. If you follow the script that you have been given and go off to separate lawyers for that purpose, you will not be left with answers to your questions, or at least answers that talk to one another. To get answers to your questions that talk to one another, you will have to go off together to one lawyer. Rather, the only thanks that you will get for having followed your script will be to have been left with different answers to the same question, which will be to be left nowhere. Nor do all of the lofty abstractions that divorce lawyers invoke in referring to legal rules change that.

If all that turning to the legal rules that the law employs will leave you with are different answers to the same question, the law will not have been of any help. Rather than solve your problem, the application of legal rules will only leave you with one. That does not represent legal sense. It is nothing but legal nonsense, and it should be labeled as such.

It is critical that you keep this distinction in mind.

CHAPTER 14

Does a Legal Question Have an Answer?

As we have seen, following your script and turning to the application of legal rules will fail four out of the five tests we agreed that any procedure you turn to for help should pass. Will it at least pass the last of those tests? In other words, even if the application of legal rules will not leave you with the right answer, will it at least leave you with an answer? This is critical. After all, if turning to the law fails all five of the tests, then you would be better off using my lowly coin. You may not have been happy with the answer that you got when you employed it—or at least one of you may not have been happy with it—and complained that I was asking you to leave the issue to chance. But my coin did leave you with the right answer half of the time. More important, whether you were happy with it or not, it did leave you with an answer every time.

I appreciate the fact that in comparing the law to a coin, it may seem as if I am parodying the law and trying to make fun of it. I am not. What would be the point in that? I am just trying to get you to see the law more realistically for what it is, namely, an arbitrary set of legal rules. I am just trying to remove the sacred halo that your script has placed around it by referring to it as representing your legal rights. If the truth be told, I was very generous to the legal rules that the law employs when I said that it was not possible for them to leave you with the right answer. I based that on the fact that rather than being universal, like the rules of mathematics, they varied from state to state. But it is worse than that. Even if those rules were the same in every state, they would still not be able to leave you with the right answer. There are many reasons for this. One will be sufficient.

I said that in the past, and except where technical knowledge was involved, you made all of the decisions in your marriage based upon your good judgment and the considerations that were important to you—what I referred to as your common sense. I went further and argued that there is absolutely no reason why you should not do the same thing now in your divorce. Since you are the ones who will have to live with whatever agreement you conclude, your common sense is enough to tell you that it should reflect the personal considerations that are important to you—how you feel.

That is not how those decisions will be made, however, if you turn to the law. The legal rules the law employs do not take into account the personal considerations that are important to you. In the terms that I have put it, if a court is called upon to decide which of you will be allowed to keep the grandfather clock, your personal feelings will have no bearing on the court's decision. That is because the law has bleached out literally all of the personal considerations that are important to you. They are not included in any of the factors the court is instructed to consider in making its determination. Thus, even if the court's decision may be the right one (as a divorce lawyer would say, "fair and equitable") in terms of the legal rules that a judge is required to employ, it will not be fair and equitable as you see it. How could it be when it will not take into account any of the personal considerations (feelings) that are important to you?

This is another unfortunate effect of a divorce lawyer's characterization of the legal rules that a court is required to apply in order to answer your questions as representing your legal rights. Legal rights are personal. They are something that belong to you. More important, they put you first. Legal rules, on the other hand, are impersonal. They have little if anything to do with you. In my terms, they do not put you first.

A divorce lawyer's characterization of legal rules denies this reality. But it denies something more, and that is the fact that legal rules are a Procrustean bed. They do not bend or accommodate themselves to fit the personal considerations that are important to you—in the terms here, how you feel. Rather, you will be forced to accommodate yourself to fit into the inflexible Procrustean bed that those legal rules represent. That is the unfortunate effect of referring to legal rules as legal rights. It disables you from being able to see this reality. The inevitable effect of this is to give you unrealistic levels of expectation when it comes to the law. You think that it is going to put you first. It isn't.

That is why I made the distinction between the questions you will have to answer and the problems you will have to solve in order to conclude an agreement, and what I meant when I said that it only made sense to look to the law to answer your questions (for example, how much the child support payment that one of you will make to the other will be) but not to solve your problems (in the terms here, who will keep the grandfather clock). Using my coin as an example will help you see this.

Following my suggestion, you decide to turn to my trusty coin to answer the question of who will keep the grandfather clock. Will it answer your question? Of course it will. Will it solve your problem? Not really. Like legal rules, my coin could not possibly take into consideration any of the feelings that are important to you. Put another way, it will have to leave one of you unhappy. To be sure, it may have solved your problem in the limited sense of answering your question. But it did not solve your problem in the larger sense of helping the two of you bring closure to this and move on with your lives. How could it if one of you felt that what he or she was left with was unfair? Again, legal rules are not capable of helping you solve your problem in that larger sense. They do not even try. Like my coin, they just answer questions.

How, then, are you going to solve the problem your grandfather clock represents, in both of those senses? It is an important question, and I will return to that at a later point. For the time being, I want to go back to the question that I posed at the beginning of this chapter. Even if the law cannot possibly provide you with the right answer to your question, will it at least leave you with an answer? That is the issue I now need to address, and it is critical. Since it will take a little time, I am going to tell you the answer in advance. The answer is no. At least if you follow the script that you have been given, and turn to separate lawyers rather than to the same lawyer to get the answers to your questions, the application of legal rules could not possibly do that. All that you will be left with is different answers. Worse, in most instances those answers will be so far apart that they will literally not talk to one another.

For the purposes of our discussion, I want to assume that the law in every state is exactly the same. In other words, the problem here is not that you will be left with different answers because you live in different states that employ different laws. After all, the two of you live in the same state. Thus, whatever attorney you consult with will be looking to the exact same legal rules. I also want to rule out the possibility that you will be left with different answers because your lawyers have different levels of training or experience, or different levels of competence. I therefore want to assume that, though you are not aware of this, you have both gone off separately and consulted with the same lawyer, one of you one week and the other the next. However, because you do not use the same last names, and because neither of you said anything that would have caused the lawyer you met with to realize that he was talking to the husband or wife of the person who consulted with him the previous week, he did not know that the two of you were married to one another. In other words, I want to make the most difficult case for myself that I can by eliminating all of the things that we would normally ascribe as being the possible reasons why the two of you might be given different answers to the same question.

Having eliminated all of those factors, won't the application of legal rules now be able to provide you with an answer to your question? The answer is still no. It has nothing to do with who is asking the question or who is answering it. (In the real world, of course, it does, but as I said, I want to eliminate that as a possible consideration.) It has to do with the fact that, unlike mathematical rules, there is no methodology when it comes to the application of legal rules. I appreciate that this will seem counterintuitive and a lot of other things as well. Nevertheless, it is true. Nor will it be difficult to demonstrate.

Why do all mathematicians give you the same answer to your question? Because they all assign the same values to the same numbers and they all follow the same procedure in dealing with those numbers. Thus, one mathematician does not say that 7 is 1 more than 5 and another that it is 4 more than 5. They all agree that it is 2 more than 5. That is because the numbers that mathematicians employ come with fixed values. Similarly, one mathematician does not say that you should add the numbers and another that you should subtract them, or one that you should multiply them and another divide them. Again all mathematicians follow the exact same procedure, which is why they will all give you the same answer, to the tenth decimal point if necessary.

As we all know, the same is not true when husbands and wives go off to separate lawyers to get answers to their questions—in my terms, to determine the answer that the application of legal rules will leave them with. No two lawyers will ever give them the same answer, even in round numbers. Rather, the answers will invariably be so far apart that they will be of absolutely no help to them. That is because, since there is no methodology to the application of legal rules, the lawyer with whom the husband consults and the lawyer with whom the wife consults can each slant the outcome in their favor.

As I said, I appreciate that this has to seem counterintuitive. Nevertheless, it is true. With that in mind, what follows is that section of New York's Domestic Relations Law which provides the factors that a court is required to consider in making an equitable distribution of the parties' marital property. (Though I am only using the law of New York as an example, what I am saying would be true of the law of every other equitable distribution state as well.)

DRL § 236

In determining an equitable disposition of property . . . the court shall consider:

1. the income and property of each party at the time of marriage, and at the time of the commencement of the action;
2. the duration of the marriage and the age and health of both parties;
3. the need of a custodial parent to occupy or own the marital residence and to use or own its household effects;
4. the loss of inheritance and pension rights upon dissolution of the marriage as of the date of dissolution;
5. any award of maintenance under subdivision six of this part;
6. any equitable claim to, interest in, or direct or indirect contribution made to the acquisition of such marital property by the party not having title, including joint efforts or expenditures and contribution and services as a spouse, parent, wage earner and homemaker, and to the career or career potential of the other party;
7. the liquid or non-liquid character of all marital property;
8. the probable future financial circumstances of each party;
9. the impossibility or difficulty of evaluating any component asset or any interest in a business, corporation or profession, and the economic desirability of retaining such asset or interest intact and free from any claim or interference by the other party;
10. the tax consequences to each party;
11. the wasteful dissipation of assets by either spouse;
12. any transfer or encumbrance made in contemplation of a matrimonial action without fair consideration;
13. any other factor which the court shall expressly find to be just and proper.

A quick reading of this statute would undoubtedly suggest that, contrary to what I have said, there is a methodology here. There isn't. There is only the illusion of one. To help you see this, I am now going to give you the recipe for my favorite salad dressing.

Recipe For Salad Dressing

For a delicious (fair and equitable) salad dressing (property distribution)mix (factor in) the following ingredients (considerations) in an electric blender (adversarial divorce proceeding)and turn it on (set it in motion)

Olive Oil
Anchovies (with oil)
Lemon Juice
Vinegar (white)
Garlic
Mustard (ground)
Sugar
Onion Salt
Celery Salt
Paprika
Blue Cheese
Worcestershire Sauce
Tobasco Sauce

You now have my recipe. Will you be able to make my salad dressing? Of course not. As with New York's Domestic Relations Law, I may have given you the ingredients. But I have not provided you with any procedure to employ in putting them together. Though you may know that you have to use both tobasco sauce and blue cheese to make my salad dressing, you do not know how much of each to throw into the blender, which is why no two chefs following my recipe will ever end up with salad dressings that taste the same. In other words, as is the case with New York's Equitable Distribution Statute, I have only given you the illusion of a methodology, not an actual one.

In the real world of cooking, we know that when you look in a cook book to get a recipe, it will tell you exactly how much of each ingredient to use in making it. Like the rules in mathematics, it will assign values to all of the ingredients. But in the real world of the law, when you look in a law book, it won't. I have given you the actual factors that the law prescribes, but they do not come with assigned values (weights). Rather, they only have such weight as a judge can be persuaded to give them. That is what the law refers to as a judge's "discretion." But unlike the recipe for my salad dressing, that discretion includes the power to not assign any weight to one or more of the factors (ingredients), which makes it even more difficult to predict what the answer will be (how it will all turn out).

But it is worse than that. My recipe may not have told you how much tobasco sauce or blue cheese to add. But it didn't leave you in the dark when it came to what tobasco sauce and blue cheese are. We all know what they are. Nor will those ingredients require any interpretation, which is why different chefs will not have any disagreement here. The same is not true, however, when it comes to the factors that a court is required to add to the mix. They do require interpretation. Take for example factor number 6, the "direct or indirect contribution made . . . to the career or career potential of the other party." Even if we knew the weight that was to be assigned to that factor (it is to be given a weight of 20%), we still have to define what that "direct or indirect contribution" was and how it affected "the career or career potential of the other party." The statute doesn't answer that question. It asks it. Moreover, since no two lawyers will ever define it (add it up) in the same way, they will never agree on what the answer is.

Unfortunately, divorcing husbands and wives who look to the law for answers to their questions do not know this. Nor will their lawyers tell them. They do not appreciate the fact that, because there is no fixed methodology to the application of legal rules, it is impossible for their respective lawyers to make any prediction as to what the answer is (how a court will decide the matter), at least any prediction that will help the two of them conclude an agreement, which was the whole point of their looking to the law in the first place. How could turning to the law possibly have done that when, because they followed their script and posed those questions to separate lawyers, they were not only left with different answers, but ones that literally did not talk to one another?

Ironically, the same would be true even if, as in the example I previously gave, they each went off separately but, unbeknownst to them, they both went off to the same attorney, but at different times. They will still come away with different answers.

I appreciate the fact that, on the face of it at least, this has to seem somewhat incredulous. After all, even if there is no fixed methodology to the application of legal rules, all that means is that, unlike mathematicians, no two lawyers will apply those rules in the same way. But certainly that does not mean that a particular lawyer will not apply those rules in the same way. And the husband and wife here both went to the same lawyer, just separately, on different days.

Nevertheless, they will still come away with different answers. Moreover, those answers will not talk to one another any better than would have been the case had they gone off to different lawyers. There are two reasons for this. The first is that they did not tell the attorney the same stories. Just as they come to their divorce with very different histories of their marriage, they also come to it with different stories. Take, for example, what they will each tell the attorney when it comes to the sixth factor that I previously mentioned, namely, the direct or indirect contributions that one of them made to the career or career potential of the other. Inevitably, they will see it very differently. Thus, one of them will tell him that their contribution accounted for everything, or almost everything. The other will tell him that it accounted for nothing, or next to nothing. The attorney in question is in no position to question their account. After all, there is no one there to take issue with it. Thus, he will have no choice but to take what he is told at face value, which is why the answer that he will give to each of them will be so different. He may have followed the same methodology in both instances, but he applied it to a totally different set of facts.

Ironically, they would have come away with different answers even if they had told him the exact same stories. Again, I appreciate the fact that this will seem incredulous. After all, the attorney in question is not in the business of misleading his clients, let alone lying to them. On the contrary, he is a very responsible practitioner. He will give them different answers nevertheless.

Again, if you do not understand this, it is because you do not understand the game you will be playing if you follow the script that you have been given. To be sure, your script will lead you to believe that the reason why you are going to an attorney is to get answers to your questions. But, as I said, while you will be asking one question, namely, what is the right answer, your attorney will be answering another, namely, what is the best answer. If that is the case, how could you possibly understand his answer? More to the point, how could you not be misled by it?

Thus, it makes no difference that the two of you will tell the attorney with whom you consult the exact same stories, down to the smallest detail. Since your attorney is an advocate, not a law professor, he will not view his function to be to take those facts and organize them so as to give you an objective picture of the law. He will view it, instead, to be to take those facts and organize them so as to make the best possible case that he can for you. And since those facts, just as those factors, do not come with assigned values, he has a great deal of leeway when it comes to that organization, which is why the answers that you will each be given will not only be different, but so different that they will literally not talk to one another.

CHAPTER 15

A Range of Possible Answers

I said that because legal rules do not come with assigned weights, there is no methodology to their application. And because there is no methodology to their application, they will not leave you with one and only one possible answer, unless that answer is the same for everyone, such as at what age someone is eligible to vote or what is the maximum speed limit on a state highway.

I appreciate that this will seem to be a criticism. It isn't. It couldn't be otherwise. With the exception of those legal rules that are meant to apply generally, and therefore be the same for everyone, our divorce laws are intended to make judgments in particular situations. In other words, the judgments that the law makes are intended to take into account the unique facts of each marriage. What that means is that since all marriages are different, the answers that the application or legal rules will leave you with will be different in every marriage.

But there is something else that accounts for the fact that the application of legal rules will not leave you with only one possible answer. After all, even if the facts in each marriage are different, once we have determined those facts, won't they add up to one and only one answer? Again the answer is no. That is because a husband's attorney and a wife's attorney are going to look at those facts very differently. To be more precise, they are going to argue that the court should look at them differently.

Admittedly, if there was only one way to look at those facts, this would not be a problem. If that were the case, legal rules would be like the rules of mathematics. They would always add up to one and only one answer.

But there isn't just one way to look at those facts. Rather, it is like the glass which some see as being half full and others as being half empty.

The parties have been married for 16 years, and the issue is what payment the husband should make to the wife for her support. To the wife, that 16 years seems like a very long time, and she feels that she should receive support for a period of at least 10 years. At least that is what her attorney is going to argue. To her husband, however, that doesn't seem like such a long time, and he feels that he should not be required to support her for more than 5 years. At least that is what his attorney is going to argue. And so it will go, right down the line.

What is the right answer here? Though divorcing husbands and wives do not appreciate this, and though their attorneys will not tell them this, there really is none. That is because, as every law student learns the first week of class, the application of legal rules does not and can not leave you with only one answer. In the terms here, they cannot leave you with the right answer. The most that they can do is leave you with a "range of possible answers," none of which are wrong.

To be sure, this is not how your attorney will present it to you. It would only confuse you, and you went to him (or her) to get an answer, not to be confused. Thus, though your attorney will not tell you this in so many words, he will nevertheless lead you to believe that there really is a right answer. There isn't. Moreover, it will be easy to prove. If there really was a right answer, your attorney should be able to write it down on a piece of paper. But he is not going to be willing to do that. How could he when there really is no methodology to the application of legal rules? How could he when he doesn't know the answer? Ironically, you are not going to ask him to do that. Though you are not aware of it, the two of you are playing a game, and putting him on the spot by asking him to write down the answer is not one of the permissible moves.

But won't it be sufficient if you are left with a range of possible answers? After all, though it would help to have the answer to the tenth decimal point, won't it be sufficient if you can at least get it in round numbers? It would be. The problem is that if you go off to separate lawyers to get those answers, you are not going to be given answers even in round numbers. Rather, the range of possible answers that you will be left with will be as wide as a mile. Thus, going off to separate lawyers to get the answers to your questions will not solve your problem. It will only leave you with one.

This brings me back to your script. I suggested that the question is not whether legal information is important. Since your common sense may not be enough to answer all of your questions, it will be. The question is how you are going to get that information. In fact, it is the critical question. That is because, whether the answer to your question is going to solve your problem or just leave you with one will depend on how you get that answer. To be sure, your script has not told you this. It does not want you to see it. After all, it was dictated by our adversarial legal system.

Let us consider this. You basically have two choices. Following your script, you can each go off to separate lawyers to get the answers to your questions. In fact, since it would not occur to you to question your script, that is what you will be inclined to do. Or you can do what you have always done in the past when you had a question the answer to which required special knowledge, which is to go off together to one lawyer.

I want to put aside for the moment the reason why your script insists that you must do something now that you would never have thought to do before. I will get to that later. For the time being I just want to indicate the necessary effect of going down one of those roads (going off to separate lawyers) rather than the other (going off to one lawyer together).

To understand this, it is necessary to return to how an adversarial divorce lawyer views his role and the function of the legal rules that he will employ in the discharge of what he considers to be his obligation to you. As I said, he is not a law professor dispensing legal information. He is an attorney—in legal terms, an advocate for a cause, that cause being you. Thus, contrary to what your script has led you to believe, he does not view his role to be to answer your questions. To be sure, he will answer them, or give you what you will mistakenly take to be answers. But that is not his primary role. Rather, it is to make a case for you. And your husband's or wife's attorney will view his or her role to be the same. Thus, in terms of the analogy of my salad dressing, if your respective attorneys are each asked how the salad dressing should be made (how much of each ingredient should be added), they are going to give you very different instructions (answers). They will appear something like this:

Wife's Attorney		Husband's Attorney
1 cup	Olive Oil	2/3 cup
2 oz.	Anchovies (with oil)	1 oz.
2 tablespoons	Lemon Juice	1 tablespoon
3 tablespoons	Vinegar (white)	1 tablespoon
4 slivers	Garlic	2 slivers
2 teaspoons	Mustard (ground)	1 teaspoon
1 tablespoon	Sugar	2 tablespoons
2 teaspoons	Onion Salt	1 teaspoon
3 teaspoons	Celery Salt	2 teaspoons
1 teaspoon	Paprika	2 teaspoons
6 oz.	Blue Cheese	3 oz.
10 drops	Worcestershire Sauce	dash
10 drops	Tobasco Sauce	5 drops

That is all well and good. But you consulted with your attorneys to get an answer, not a debate going nowhere as to what the answer is or should be. How are the two of you going to make the salad dressing here (conclude an agreement) based on the different instructions that each of your attorneys has given to you? You are not. The fact that your attorneys characterized their instructions in terms of lofty abstractions ("the best salad dressing in the world") does not mean that what you were told helped the two of you answer your questions—in my terms, that it represented legal sense. It was nothing but legal nonsense. It was nothing but a waste of time. Again, you do not need more than your common sense to tell you this.

This brings us back to the range of possible answers that the application of legal rules will provide you with. It would not be a criticism of legal rules that their application could not leave you with an answer that was correct to the tenth decimal point, as would be the case when it came to the application of mathematical rules. It wouldn't be a criticism because, in terms of why you are looking to those rules, it wouldn't matter. Thus, it will not necessarily leave you with a problem if one of you was told that the answer is 20 (that is how much you should receive) and the other that the answer is 18 (that is how much you should give). The two of you would still be able to come to an agreement. It is called 19. After all, we are all brought up to compromise.

But suppose, instead, one of you is told the answer is 25 (you are legally entitled to at least that) and the other is told the answer is 15 (that you do not have a legal obligation to give any more than that). Where does that leave you? Nowhere. There is nothing that you can do with those two numbers. In my terms, they do not talk to one another. That is because there is no number in between that you could settle on that would not leave one of you, and probably both of you, coming away feeling a fool. Nevertheless, that is exactly where you will be left if, following the script you have been given, you go off to separate lawyers to get those answers.

Why will you be left with such different answers—in the terms here, such a large range of answers—if you each go off to separate lawyers to get those answers rather than together to one lawyer? This is something else that you will not find any mention of in your script. Nevertheless, it is critical in terms of understanding how and for what purpose legal rules are employed in adversarial divorce proceedings. What I am going to argue is that it is in the very nature of an adversarial legal system to expand the range of possible answers.

In that connection, it must be remembered what a divorce lawyer's role is. As I said, it is not to answer your questions, though that is what you think that he or she is doing. It is to make a case for you, the best possible case that he can. To make the best possible case that he can means, of necessity, to push the limits of the law. Thus, to make the best possible case that he can, one of your attorneys will push the limits on one side of the range of possible answers and the other will push the limits on the other side. The necessary effect of this will be to expand the range of possible answers. That is what I mean when I say that the answers you will be given if you turn to separate lawyers will literally not talk to one another. How could they when they will be miles apart?

But it is not just that your respective lawyers will be trying to push the limits of the law in your particular case that tends to expand the range of possible answers. It is that adversarial divorce lawyers generally like a wide range of possible answers. In fact, they will resist any attempt to narrow the range of possible answers.

In that regard, a divorce lawyer is like a running back in football. A running back's job is to bring the ball down the field, hopefully into the end zone. To do that, he is going to need as much running room as he can get. A playing field 15 feet wide is not going to do that. It will not give him anywhere to go—give him enough room to show off his skills as a running back. In order for him to be able to do that, he will want and need a much wider playing field.

The same is true of a divorce lawyer. If the latitude of the law (the range of possible answers) was only between 18 and 20, that would seriously restrict a divorce lawyer's ability to make a case for a client. There would be no place for him to go. In fact, no one would ever hire a divorce lawyer if the law was that clear. What would be the point of that? So, like a running back in football, a divorce lawyer is going to want and need a much larger playing field—range of possible answers.

To be sure, that may serve a divorce lawyer's purpose in the sense of enabling him to make the best possible case that he can for his client. But it will not serve your purpose, and why you looked to the application of legal rules in the first place, which was to help you conclude an agreement. That is because the wider the range of possible answers that the application of legal rules will leave you with, the less effective those answers will be for that purpose. Put another way, they will serve a divorce lawyer's purpose better than they will serve yours. That is also something that your script has not told you.

With that in mind, let me go back to the couple who have been married for 16 years. The wife's attorney has suggested that she should receive support for at least 10 years. The husband's attorney has suggested that he should not be required to pay it for more than 5 years. Perhaps that is close enough. After all, they could agree on 7-1/2 years. But that is not the end of it. The wife's attorney has also suggested that she should receive support of $5,000 per month. For his part, the husband's attorney has suggested that he should not be required to pay more than $3,000 per month.

At first blush, that may still not seem that far apart. When you do the math, however, you will see that it is miles apart. The wife's attorney is suggesting that the wife should receive support totaling $600,000. The husband's attorney is suggesting that the husband should only be required to pay support totaling $180,000. That is a much bigger difference. But we are not done doing the math. After all, I have only mentioned two of the questions that the two of them will have to answer. There will be many more. Moreover, the answers that they will be given by their respective attorneys will be just as far apart when it comes to each of them. When those different answers are also factored into the equation, that will only make their ability to conclude an agreement that much more difficult. In fact, it will make it all but impossible.

That is what you can expect if you follow the script that you have been given and go off to separate lawyers. As countless numbers of husbands and wives who have made that mistake will tell you, the only thanks you will get will be to be left with answers that literally do not talk to one another. You will be left nowhere. It will not be possible for your attorneys to satisfy both of you. The irony is that they will not be able to satisfy either of you. How could they when they have given you such different answers when it comes to what you have a right to expect?

That raises the obvious question. How are your two lawyers going to solve the problem that they have created for you? What your script would have you believe is that, based on their knowledge of the law and their skill as attorneys, they are somehow going to find a way out of the mess that they have created. Again, like so much else that your script would have you believe, that is simply legal nonsense. Your common sense should be enough to tell you this. Their knowledge and skill will have nothing to do with it. How could it when the answers they have given each of you are so far apart that it has left them with literally nothing to talk about? Thus, if the two of you eventually come to an agreement, your attorneys' skills and effort will have little to do with it. Rather, it will be brought about by attrition. Finally, when the two of you are so worn down, so emotionally exhausted, and so financially drained, you will give up and give in. As divorce lawyers say, you will "settle" the case, which is a polite way to say that you will end up paying more or receiving less then you were led to believe you were legally obligated or entitled to.

Unfortunately, there is a price to be paid for this. Again, you will not find any mention of it in your script. That price is that you are going to be left more hurt, more angry and with more of a sense that you were made to suffer a terrible injustice, than you were when you began. Divorce lawyers have an expression for this. As they say, divorces never end. Rather, your agreement will now just become the battlefield on which you will wage your future wars.

CHAPTER 16

It's the System

I have argued that if you follow the script you have been given and go off to separate lawyers to get the answers to your questions, your attorneys are not going to give it to you straight. Unlike a mathematician, who will apply mathematical rules objectively, without any concern as to the answer he gives to you other than that it be the right one, a divorce lawyer is a biased observer. He has a dog in that fight. And because he is a biased observer, he is not going to apply legal rules objectively. Rather, he is going to slant their application to get the most favorable answer that he can for one of you, namely his client.

Would a divorce lawyer take exception to this? No. On the contrary, he would be proud of it. All that I have done is describe his ethical obligation, which is to be an advocate for the interests of his client alone and to allow no other competing interest or concern to distract him.

This, of course, is the way your script describes a divorce lawyer's role and it is a very flattering description, which is why no divorce lawyer would take exception to it. It portrays him as a knight in shining armor prepared to take up arms on behalf of someone in distress and in need of protection, namely his client. That is not how it plays, however. He is not a knight in shining armor. In the adversarial world in which your divorce will take place if you follow that script, he is just a hired gun, and he will shoot in whatever direction he has been paid to shoot. Admittedly, your script has not described his role in these less than flattering terms. Why would you expect it to? After all, it was written by divorce lawyers.

This raises a question. Am I telling it to you straight? In other words, is my less than flattering description fair to divorce lawyers? It isn't and it is.

I personally know many divorce lawyers for whom I have nothing but the utmost respect. They are highly skilled practitioners. They sincerely belive that all they are doing is trying to secure their clients legal rights and leave them with an agreement that is fair and equitable. Moreover, since they are responsible lawyers, they would be very taken aback if they thought that there was any truth to my suggestion that they are not telling it straight when it comes to the application of legal rules. They would be even more taken aback at my characterization of them as being nothing more than hired guns. In fact, they would insist that they are not only applying those rules, and conducting themselves, in a completely ethical manner, but also in strict conformity with the Code of Professional Responsibility which they have sworn to uphold. And they would be right. If that is so, how can my characterization possibly be correct? In fact, how can it be anything other than irresponsible? Unfortunately, it is correct and it isn't irresponsible.

Divorcing husbands and wives simply do not and cannot understand how deep the waters that they are wading into are when they turn to adversarial divorce proceedings. They are so taken in by the window dressing that they accept it all at face value. Divorce lawyers characterize the undertaking as being one to secure their legal rights and to leave them with an agreement that is fair and equitable, and they uncritically accept that and brush everything else under the carpet. To be sure, they know that there are problems. How could they not know that when they see it all around them? Nevertheless, they persist in the illusion that it is simply because there are a few bad apples (lawyers) who are contaminating the barrel. All that we have to do is remove those bad apples and everything will be fine.

It won't be. To be sure, there are a few bad apples in the barrel. There are a few bad apples in every barrel. But the problem isn't that these few bad apples are contaminating the barrel. It is that the barrel is contaminating the apples. That is why, in answer to the question whether my characterization was fair to divorce lawyers, I said that it isn't and it is. It makes no difference that most divorce lawyers are responsible practitioners. They are still responsible attorneys who practice in an irresponsible system.

As I said earlier, ours is not a friendly legal system. It is anything but that. Nor do divorce lawyers apologize for that. On the contrary, they are very proud of it—proud that ours is an adversarial legal system, as they consider that to be its principal virtue. But that is also the problem. Contrary to the window dressing that induces husbands and wives to turn to divorce lawyers, an adversarial divorce proceeding is not a search for the truth. Nor is it a proceeding whose purpose is to leave them with the right answer. Rather, it is a form of legal warfare where the object is simply to get as much as you can and to give as little as you have to—a game of legal chess, if you will—where legal rules rather than guns are the instruments that are used to advance each of the parties' cause. Thus, it makes no difference that, like Robert E. Lee, a divorce lawyer may be the finest gentleman the South ever produced. War makes killers of us all and his bullets will do the job as well as anyone else's.

It is in that sense my characterization of a divorce lawyer's role was both correct and a fair one. People are what they do, and if what someone does is kill people, then he is a killer. He is no less a killer because his name is Robert E. Lee. Similarly, the object of an adversarial divorce proceeding is not to get the right answer. It is to get the best answer. And what is best answer? It is to get as much as you can and to give as little as you have to.

It is amazing, knowing what we all know about adversarial divorce proceedings, that divorcing husbands and wives do not see this. It is amazing that, taken in by all of the lofty abstractions, they buy into the rather incredible suggestion that turning to an adversarial divorce proceeding—taking what is obviously a serious problem and making a game of it—is an appropriate, let alone responsible, way to deal with the tragedy which their divorce represents. It isn't. It is nothing but legal warfare, which means that, like all warfare, it is a form of institutional insanity.

To be sure, there are some wars that we have no choice but to fight. Few of us would argue that World War II was not one of them. But you do not fight wars that you do not have to. You certainly do not fight wars that you can prevent. Thus, contrary to what divorce lawyers would have you believe, the fact that the two of you have differences of opinion when it comes to the questions that you have to answer and the problems that you have to solve does not mean that the two of you are adversaries. It certainly does not mean that you must engage in hand-to-hand legal combat with one another to resolve them. Nor do all of the lofty abstractions that divorce lawyers invoke to persuade you otherwise—that the object of the undertaking is to protect your legal rights and secure an agreement that is fair and equitable—change that. They just induce you to follow the script you have been given, take up arms and do mindless battle with one another. They just disable you from being able to see what you are not supposed to see, namely, that this is simply legal nonsense and dangerous nonsense at that.

You cannot afford to be taken in by all of these lofty abstractions. If you do, you will suffer the fate that the countless number of divorcing husbands and wives who made the mistake of following that script did. As they learned to their regret, all that it did was send them off on a fool's errand in search of fool's gold. All that it did is leave them coming back empty handed. Needless to say, you do not want that to be your fate.

CHAPTER 17

A Legal Answer Is Not There Just For The Asking

When we ask a question, we assume there is an answer to it. Thus, if we ask when the Battle of Hastings took place or when the Magna Carta was signed, we expect to be given an answer. More important, we expect that the answer will be the right one. All that we have to do is ask the right person (a professor of English history) or go to the right place (a history book or the internet). That will be the end of it. We will be told that the Battle of Hastings took place in 1066 and that the Magna Carta was signed in 1215. The answer was there just for the asking.

That is not true of all questions, however. You cannot just open a book to get the answer. Rather, you will have to follow a procedure. That, of course, is the case with mathematical questions. If you want the answer that the application of mathematical rules will give you, then you are going to have to follow the procedure that mathematics provides to get it. To be sure, if you ask a mathematician how much 7 times 6 is, he will not need to follow any procedure. Like the professor of English history, he will be able to give you the answer from memory. However, if the question is more complicated—for example, the square root of 1,323,484—no mathematician would be able to give you the answer from memory. In other words, it is not there just for the asking. Rather, it is the endpoint of a procedure, and the only way to get the answer is to follow the procedure that you have been given to get it.

Though divorcing husbands and wives do not appreciate this as they should, the same is true when it comes to the answers that they will be en by the application of legal rules. Those answers are not there just for the asking. To be sure, as with the question of how much 7 times 6 is, there are some legal questions where that is the case. Thus, if a teenager asks a lawyer at what age he can vote, the lawyer will not be required to turn to the application of legal rules in order to give him an answer. The answer is age 18 and he knows it from memory.

Unfortunately, divorcing husbands and wives get misled by this. They also get misled by the fact that the attorney with whom they consulted gave them an answer—or at least what they took to be an answer—to almost any question they asked. Thus, they were led to believe that there are answers to all of their legal questions. Moreover, since the attorney with whom they consulted seemed to be giving those answers to them off the top of his head, from memory, they could not help but also conclude that a legal answer is there just for the asking.

It isn't. The only time that a lawyer can give you an answer to a question just for the asking is when, like the age at which someone can vote, the answer is the same for everyone. That is not the case, however, when it comes to the questions that husbands and wives turn to lawyers to answer. As we have seen, the answers will be dependent upon the particular facts of each marriage. And since no two marriages are exactly the same, the answers will be different in each instance.

This will be evident if you go back to Chapter 14 and look at the factors that a court in New York is required to take into account in determining what would be an appropriate distribution of the parties' marital property. Neither the law of New York nor of any other state has a set of factors that must be taken into account in order to determine at what age someone can obtain a driver's license. The answer there doesn't depend on a set of factors. It just depends on the person's age. But, like other states, the law of New York does have a list of factors that must be taken into account in determining what would constitute an appropriate (equitable) distribution of their marital property. The same is true when it comes to the payment that one of them will be required to make to the other for his or her support. In other words, the answer is not the same for everyone. Rather, it depends on the particular circumstances of each marriage. As we say, no two cases are the same.

Divorcing husbands and wives do not appreciate this as they should. They get so taken in by the fact that the lawyer with whom they consulted gave them answers to their questions or, as I said, what they mistakenly took to be answers, that they think that is all there is to it. It isn't. It is because the answers that their husband or wife were given by the attorney with whom they consulted were very different.

To be sure, divorcing husbands and wives know that their lawyers are going to give them different answers to the same questions. Nevertheless, they do not give as much thought to this as they should. In fact, they do not think about it at all. After all, their lawyer told them what the law is. If their husband or wife says they were told something different, that is just evidence of their bad faith. The script that they are following warned them of this.

Ironically, it doesn't make any difference whether what their husband or wife tells them represents bad faith or whether it is simply what they were told by their own attorney. In either case, the two of them have been left with different answers to the same questions. In other words, the fact that the attorneys with whom they each consulted gave them answers to their questions didn't end the matter. How could it when they were each given such different answers—as I characterized it, answers that literally do not talk to one another?

That, of course, is exactly where you will be left if you follow your script and go off to separate lawyers to get the answers to your questions. You will be left nowhere. You will be left exactly where you started out. How, then, will you get the answers to your questions? Since a legal answer is not there just for the asking—since it is the endpoint of a procedure—there is only one way. You will have to follow the procedure that the law provides to get that answer.

That procedure, of course, is an adversarial one. That is what it means to say that ours is an adversarial legal system. Thus, since your two attorneys are not going to agree on what the answer is, you are going to have to go to court—to the court of last resort—to get it. To be sure, your script has not told you this. As I said, you will not even find it in the fine print at the end. You don't have to be told. You know it.

Obviously, that is not what either of you want. How, then, can you avoid it? Your common sense will be enough to tell you. The only reason why you are going to have to resort to the procedure that the law provides to get an answer to a legal question is that you have each been given different answers—as I put it, answers that do not talk to one another. That is because you turned to separate lawyers to get those answers. If you want the same answer, one which will avoid your having to go to court to get it, you will have to go off together to one lawyer to get it.

I said that the only time that a legal answer is there just for the asking is when the answer is the same for everyone. The example that I gave was the age at which someone can obtain a driver's license. Haven't I prejudiced the issue? Aren't there other questions, less universal, to which there really are legal answers just for the asking? There are and there aren't.

To help you better understand this, I will tell you about another disagreement that Mark and Susan are having. Just before they bought their home, Susan's father made a gift to her of $100,000. He gave her a check in that amount made payable to her, which she then deposited in a checking account in her name. At the closing, she issued her check to the sellers in that amount in partial payment of the purchase price. Title to the home was taken in her and Mark's joint names.

Susan feels that upon the sale of the home that amount should be returned to her before she and Mark divide the balance of the proceeds. Clearly the $100,000 was a gift to her alone and, as such, she feels that she should keep it. Mark disagrees. When Susan used the $100,000 that her father had given to her to purchase their home, she made a gift of half of that amount to Mark. What is she, an Indian giver? Besides, the gift was intended to help the two of them buy their home, title to which Susan's father knew was going to be taken in their joint names. What difference, therefore, did it make to whom the check was made payable?

Mark has other arguments as well. As he said, this is just one of many contributions that they each made to their marriage. One of the contributions that he brought to the marriage was his greater earning ability, which resulted in the money they saved while they were married that was also used to buy their home. Why should Susan's contribution be singled out for special treatment?

Let us suppose that instead of having the good sense to go off together to Justin Wright, Susan and Mark had followed their script and gone off to separate lawyers to get an answer to their question. What would Susan's lawyer have told her? He would have told her that she was legally entitled to the return of the $100,000.

What would Mark's lawyer have told him? Let us assume that the law in the state in which they live would credit Susan with this $100,000. (In technical terms, the law would hold that since the money represented a gift to Susan alone, it constituted her separate property and that it did not lose its character as such because she then used it to purchase a home title to which was taken in her and Mark's joint names.) Let us further assume that Mark's lawyer knows this as well as Susan's lawyer does. Will he tell Mark that Susan is entitled to the return of the $100,000?

More important, will he send Susan's lawyer a letter telling him that he concedes that Susan is entitled to the return of the money? After all, Mark has retained him to conclude an agreement between Susan and himself and this would tend to narrow the issues between the two of them and get them closer to an agreement.

The answer is no on both counts. To be sure, Mark's lawyer thinks that there is a lot of merit to Mark's argument. Each of them did make numerous contributions to their marriage. Why should this one of Susan's be singled out for special treatment? In the terms that a divorce lawyer would put it, is that fair?

Unfortunately, fair, like beauty is in the eye of the beholder. Thus, it depends upon how you look at it, in this case how the court will look at it. Susan's lawyer obviously thinks the answer is very clear. Mark's lawyer actually does as well. The court is not very likely to look at all of those other contributions when it comes to deciding what will happen to Susan's contribution of $100,000. Rather, it will treat it on its own. And if it does, it will credit Susan with it.

Why then won't Mark's lawyer admit this? There are many reasons. The first is that Mark has a very good argument. To be sure, it may not be legally relevant. But that does not mean that it is not personally relevant, and if what Mark and Susan are supposedly trying to do is conclude an agreement that is fair and equitable, why should Mark's contribution not be factored in as well? Besides, they are not in court yet. They are still negotiating, and the fact that Mark's argument may not be relevant in a court of law doesn't mean that Mark's attorney can not press it in the negotiations, perhaps in return for something else.

The second reason is that Mark's attorney is guided by a maxim that tells him not to concede or admit anything. To be sure, that maxim would not make any sense if, like mathematical rules, the application of legal rules represented a fixed procedure which will leave you with one and only one right answer. But it doesn't, which is why he thinks that it makes sense to be guided by that maxim. What it tells him is, "Hey, you never know." Or, as he says, "I have seen worse arguments fly," and so has every other lawyer. After all, is there a major horse race that has not been won, if only once, by a 40-to-1 longshot?

But there is a third reason as well. Let us suppose that in this instance the odds are even less than that. In other words, let us assume that, when it gets down to it, Mark's lawyer is not going to try to make a case that Susan should not get a credit for this $100,000. That still leaves the same question. What would be the point in Mark's attorney conceding that? What will Mark get for it? To be more accurate, what will Susan's lawyer be willing to give him for it? Absolutely nothing. To be sure, Mark's lawyer may not press the issue with Susan's lawyer. He may not even mention it, at least at this point. That might only tend to cause Susan's lawyer to conclude that he is not acting in good faith and there is no point in talking to him. But he is not going to spend too much time discussing this with Mark either. Rather, he is going to go on to other things. What that means of course is that the matter will not be over just because Mark and Susan went off to separate lawyers and got answers to their questions even when, as here, the answer is pretty clear. They are still going to be left with the reality that a legal answer is the endpoint of a process. They are still going to have to play the game.

CHAPTER 18

Getting an Answer—Making a Case

I said that divorcing husbands and wives do not appreciate as they should that a legal answer is not there just for the asking. There is something else that they do not appreciate. Admittedly, this is going to surprise you. Since divorcing husbands and wives go to a lawyer in order to get answers to their questions, and since the lawyer they met with gave them answers, or what they took to be answers, it is understandable that they assumed that it was a lawyer's role, namely, to answer their questions concerning the law.

Unfortunately, this is another example of where your script has misled you. Contrary to what it would have you believe, a divorce lawyer does not view his role to be to answer your questions. As I said, he is not a law professor. He is an advocate. Thus, he views his role to be to make a case for you, the best possible case that he can. The result is that while husbands and wives are asking their attorney one question—what is the right answer?—their attorney is answering another—what is the best answer? We saw that when it came to the contribution of $100,000 that Susan made to the purchase of her and Mark's home. The right answer—at least the legally right answer—was that Susan was entitled to a credit for that $100,000, and if Mark had posed that question to a law professor, that is what he would have been told. But he didn't pose it to a law professor. He posed it to a divorce lawyer, and for a divorce lawyer (at least his divorce lawyer) that was not the best answer. How could it be when, in completely ignoring Mark's contribution, it didn't leave him with the answer he wanted and thought he deserved?

In order for you to better understand this, I need to return to what I said earlier was the difference between an attorney and a mathematician. A mathematician employs mathematical rules to solve a problem and answer a question. Thus, if a husband and wife have a difference of opinion as to how much one of them owes the other and turn to a mathematician to get an answer, the mathematician may know that one of them is hoping that the answer will be a large number and the other that it will be a small number. But what difference does that make? It is what it is, and a mathematician is not going to prejudice the outcome by applying the rules of mathematics just to make one of them happy. Rather, he is going to apply them impartially, exactly as they have been given to him. Moreover, the two of them are going to have to live with the answer he gives them, whether they like it or not.

A divorce lawyer is not a legal mathematician. Unlike a mathematician, he is not an unbiased observer. Rather, he is an advocate for his client. More important, his role is to do whatever he can to advance his client's interests. That is his ethical obligation and he has sworn to uphold it. Thus, a divorce lawyer is not going to apply legal rules to get the right answer. He would not even know what that means. He is going to apply them to get the best answer—to make the best possible case that he can for one of them, his client. Where will that leave his client's husband or wife, of even his client's children? That is not a lawyer's concern.

But there is another reason why divorce lawyers are not going to tell it to you straight—why, if you and your husband or wife go off to separate lawyers, you will be given different answers to the same question. Unlike a mathematician, your lawyers want to make you happy. That is what you are paying them to do.

As we have seen, a mathematician could not care less whether you will like the answer he gives to you. His only concern is that the answer is the correct one. Besides, what could you do if you do not like his answer? Go and pose the question to another mathematician? It wouldn't make any difference if you posed it to twenty mathematicians. They will all give you the same answer.

The same is not true when it comes to the application of legal rules, however. That is why, if you pose the question to twenty different lawyers, you will get twenty different answers. Nor is it possible to prove that any of them are wrong. How could you when there is no fixed methodology to the application of legal rules? How could you if your lawyers are able to assign just about any weight they wish to those factors? What that means is if you are not happy with the answer the lawyer you consulted with gives to you, you can always go off and consult with another lawyer who may give you one that you like better. And, unlike a mathematician, your attorney knows this.

In the adversarial world of divorce, this cannot help but affect the answer that a divorce lawyer will give to you. Understandably, divorcing husbands and wives are somewhat overwhelmed by anxiety at the prospect of their divorce and fearful when it comes to the future. As a result, they are more likely to listen to someone who tells them what they want to hear than to someone who doesn't. Divorce lawyers know this. Thus, the only thanks that they may get in telling it to you straight is that you may go and find a lawyer who will tell you something that is more in keeping with what you want to hear.

That is what I meant when I said that if you follow your script and go off to separate lawyers to get the answers to your questions, you are going to be asking one question and your attorney answering another. The question that you will be asking is, if the outcome is left to the application of legal rules, what will be the answer? The question that your attorney will be answering is, if I am able to bend the legal rules that I have been given to your advantage, what is the best case that I will be able to make for you. That is why you have misunderstood your attorney's answer. You thought he was answering your question. He wasn't. He was answering his own.

To be sure, divorce lawyers do not publicly advertise this fact. It wouldn't play very well. Better to say that their object is to protect your legal rights and get what is fair and equitable. Better to say that, towards that end, they will devote their efforts to assure that you will be provided with a level playing field. But that is all just window dressing. Notwithstanding all of the high sounding talk, unlike a mathematician, a divorce lawyer is going to do whatever he can to slant the playing field, and the outcome, in his client's favor. As a professor from Harvard Law School put it in reference to the defense of a criminal case, "A criminal trial is anything but a pure search for truth. When defense attorneys represent guilty clients—as most do, most of the time—their responsibility is to try, by all fair and ethical means, to prevent the truth about their client's guilt from emerging. Failure to do so . . . . is malpractice." What is true of a criminal trial is no less true when it comes to the trial of a matrimonial action. As I said, a divorce lawyer is not interested in getting the right answer. He wants to get the best answer. After all, that is what he has been paid to do.

But isn't that what you want your lawyer to do? Don't you want him to make the best possible case that he can for you? Unfortunately, it is not as simple as that. If you look to a divorce lawyer for that purpose, your husband or wife will do the same thing. You will have left them no choice. After all, the best possible case for one of you is the worst possible case for the other. Thus, having issued a declaration of war, you will have left them with no choice but to join you in doing legal battle. That is the thanks that you will get if you follow the script you have been given.

CHAPTER 19

Making Informed, Intelligent Decisions

Why is it necessary for you to consult with a lawyer before you make any of the decisions in your divorce? What your script will tell you is that you must do that to assure that the decisions you make will be informed, intelligent ones. Like most things in that script, that seems reasonable enough, at least if you do not give too much thought to it, which you are not supposed to. The minute you do, however, like most things in that script, it doesn't make very much sense. In fact, it is little more than doubletalk.

What is that script really telling you? It is saying that it is not possible for you to make an informed, intelligent decision when it comes to the questions that you are faced with unless and until you have first determined what answers the application of legal rules will leave you with. Why is that? After all, as we saw earlier when it came to the decision that you made with respect to the payment of your children's college education expenses, you made all of the decisions in your marriage without first determining that. Does that mean that none of those decisions were informed, intelligent ones? Not even a divorce lawyer would suggest that.

But that was in your marriage. This is now your divorce. I want to put aside the fact that a divorce lawyer would not be able to give you a good reason why this makes any difference. In other words, I want to assume that even if it was not necessary to know what answers to your questions the application of legal rules would have left you with in your marriage, it is essential that you know that in your divorce. Unfortunately, that concession does not end the matter. That still leaves you with all of the problems inherent in the application of legal rules, the principal one being that, in most cases at least, they do not leave you with any answer, let alone the right one. How does a divorce lawyer deal with that? He doesn't. Again, that is where all the lofty abstractions come in. Instead of saying that it is important that you know what answers the application of legal rules will leave you with, he distracts your attention by sanctifying those answers. They are not just answers to your questions. They are your legal rights, and it is important that you know what they are. Who could quarrel with that?

Needless to say, changing the description doesn't change the problem. Nor does it solve it. Regardless of how you describe what is at issue, in both cases you still don't know the answer. The attorney you consulted with didn't tell you. To be more accurate, he didn't tell you the whole story. That is because he only showed you a narrow portion of the range of possible answers, the portion most favorable to you, not the entire range. He didn't show you that portion of the range of possible answers that your husband or wife was shown by their attorney.

Where is that going to leave you? It will certainly not leave the two of you in a position to conclude an agreement. How could it when the answers you were each given are so far apart that they literally do not talk to one another? What then will you do? You will do what all divorcing husbands and wives who make the mistake of following their script do. The two of you (really your attorneys) will play a game of legal chess.

Suppose that you do not want to make a game out of this. Suppose that you really do want to be able to make an informed, intelligent decision. In the terms here, suppose that you want to come away with the whole range of possible answers—not just the portion most favorable to you but also the portion less favorable to you. How could you do that?

Actually, that would not be too difficult. Each of you could accompany the other when he or she goes off to consult with their attorney. Unfortunately, while this makes far more sense than your script would have you believe, neither of your attorneys will feel comfortable with this. In fact they will not allow it. That is not how the game is played.

That only leaves you with your own attorney. How can you get him to give you a picture of the whole range of possible answers, not just the narrow portion of it most favorable to you? One thing that you might do would be to ask him to tell you what answers he would have given to your husband or wife had they, rather than you, consulted with him. After all, since your attorney represents both husbands and wives, he could just as easily have answered their questions as he did yours. You aren't going to ask your attorney to do that, however. You and he may be playing a game, but neither of you wants to acknowledge that, and suggesting that he tell you what he would have told your husband or wife would get too close to that. After all, implicit in what you are asking him to do is the suggestion that, on different occasions, he talks out of different sides of his mouth. That may be true, but that doesn't mean that you want to imply that. It runs the risk of turning your attorney, who is supposed to be on your side, into your adversary.

There is another, less threatening way. You could tell your attorney that you have to assume that your husband or wife already has, or shortly will, consult with their own attorney. You also have to assume that their attorney will give them different answers to their questions than he has given to you. It would help you to know what their attorney will tell them.

Your attorney will not answer this question either, even though it is a perfectly reasonable one. He is not constitutionally capable of answering it. He does not and cannot think that way. In fact, as reasonable as the question is, the fact that you would ask it means that you do not understand the game that you and your attorney are playing. You certainly do not know what an adversarial divorce proceeding is.

When you follow the script that you have been given, whether you are aware of it or not, you are not only asking your attorney to put your interests first, but also to completely ignore the interests of your husband or wife, and even those of your children. Your husband or wife is of absolutely no account. In fact, in terms of your attorney's role, they do not exist except as obstacles to what is best for you. Thus, for your attorney to consider them, even to think about them, would be a breach of his professional responsibility to you.

To be sure, you have not said this to your attorney—that he is to treat your husband or wife as being of no account. Nor has he said this to you in so many words. Nevertheless, that is the game that you and he are playing. That is why he is constitutionally incapable of answering the question that I suggested you could put to him, as reasonable as it might be. To answer it would require him to do the very thing that he is not allowed to do, namely, to be objective—in the terms that I have put it, to put himself not only in your shoes but also in the shoes of your husband or wife.

Unfortunately, that is not the end of the game that you and your attorney are playing. Though you will not realize this when you leave his office, your attorney will not really have given you any answers to your questions, at least any answers that you can go to the bank with. To be sure, he will have explained the law to you and what you can expect very professionally. He will even have gone into it in great detail. Nevertheless, you will not really understand very much of what he said. You may even have found it somewhat overwhelming and more than a little confusing. Thus, you will come away with very little that is definite—very little that you can write down on a piece of paper. To be sure, your attorney may have told you that, when it comes to your home, upon its sale the proceeds will be divided equally between the two of you. But you knew that, or at least assumed it, before you met with him. It is the all the rest that you do not know, for example, whether you will be entitled to receive support from your husband or wife (or pay support to them) and, if so, how much and for how long. Your attorney will not really have answered that question except in very general terms. He certainly will not give you a letter telling you what you have a right to expect—what you can bank on.

But that still leaves you without any answer. Though you followed the instructions in your script, you are still unable to make an informed, intelligent decision. One way to solve that problem would be to tell your attorney that you know that it is not possible for him to tell you exactly how much you will receive (or be required to pay) and for precisely how long. Nevertheless, it would help you if he would at least give you some general idea. With that, you could then take out a summary that you prepared before coming to meet with him. In one column, you have listed all of the possible amounts that you could receive or be required to pay. In the other you have listed all of the possible periods of time that you could receive or be required to pay it. It would look like this:

Amounts of Money	Periods of Time
More than $10,000 per month	More than 20 years
$10,000	20 years
$ 9,500	19 years
$ 9,000	18 years
$ 8,500	17 years
$ 8,000	16 years

$ 7,500	15 years
$ 7,000	14 years
$ 6,500	13 years
$ 6,000	12 years
$ 5,500	11 years
$ 5,000	10 years
$ 4,500	9 years
$ 4,000	8 years
$ 3,500	7 years
$ 3,000	6 years
$ 2,500	5 years
Less than $2,500 per month	Less than 5 years

Having given him this summary, you could say that you know that he can not tell you what the maximum amounts or periods of time will be (if you will be the one receiving the payment) or what the minimum amounts or periods of time will be (if you will be the one making the payment). Thus, all that you are asking him to do is circle what the minimum amounts and periods of time will be (if you will be the one receiving the payment) or what the maximum amounts or periods of time will be (if you will be the one making the payment).

That is not really too much to ask. While he may not be able to tell you what is the most or least that you can expect (depending upon whether you are the one making the payment or receiving it), he should at least be able to tell you what the minimum or maximum amounts and periods of time will be. What does it mean to say that he is qualified to answer your questions about the law if he is not able to do that? Nevertheless, he will not be willing to tell you. It will put him on the spot. If he tells you a number that you will be happy with, he runs the risk that he may not be able to get it for you. On the other hand, if plays it safe and gives you a different number, one that you will be less happy with, he runs the risk of losing you as a client. You may go and find another attorney, one who will give you an answer that you like better.

What will your attorney's response be? One possibility is that he will end the meeting. As I said previously, as reasonable as your request may be, it still runs the risk of suggesting that you do not completely trust him, thereby turning him into your adversary. Besides, being a divorce lawyer is difficult enough as it is. No divorce lawyer wants to make it more difficult by having an impossible client, and that is how he may begin to view you.

Another possibility is he will tell you that it is not possible for him to give you an answer at this time. This is just an initial consultation and there is still too much he does not know. Nor will he learn what he needs to know in order to properly answer your questions until you have retained him and he has had an opportunity to do his homework—as a divorce lawyer characterizes it, to conduct his discovery and inspection.

Is that a fair answer? It is and it isn't. It is in the sense that your attorney may be quite right when he says there is more he needs to know in order to properly answer your question. In fact, in many instances it would be irresponsible for him to answer it at this point. He would be doing nothing but shooting from the hip, and you deserve better than that.

Nevertheless, in an important sense it is not a fair answer, for a number of reasons. The first is that in most instances there is really very little that he needs to know that he does not already know. You have told him that. You are not captains of industry. You are both employed with fixed salaries and your principal assets are the equity in your home and your retirement benefits. To be sure, he may go through the motions of having his discovery and inspection. But that is just because it is what divorce lawyers do. They always proceed on the assumption that there are hidden assets somewhere. But they will not really know any more when they get through than they do now. Most husbands and wives are an open book.

It is not a fair answer for another reason. If it is not possible for a divorce lawyer to answer your questions unless and until he has conducted his discovery and inspection, on what basis did he answer your questions when you first met with him? He certainly did not answer each and every question that you asked by saying, "I cannot answer that at this point. I first have to conduct my discovery and inspection."

But it is not a fair answer even in those cases where, because you and your husband or wife are not an open book (you own your own business or professional practice, your finances are very complicated, etc.) he could not properly answer your questions unless and until he has completed his discovery and inspection. When he said that, he nevertheless led you to believe that, though he could not properly answer your question now, he would be willing and able to do that at a later point—in the terms here, that if you give him the summary that you prepared of the amounts and lengths of time after he has conducted his discovery and inspection, he will be willing to tell you the least or most amounts of time and money that you can expect to receive or be required to pay. But when it comes down to it, he won't be willing to do that, which is why I said that his answer is still not a fair one.

As I said, whether you are aware of it or not, you and your attorney are playing a bit of a game. Regardless of when you give it to him, the summary that you prepared will still have the effect of giving away that game. That is why it made him feel uncomfortable. It is also why he will not give you an answer either now or later. It is going to require him to put his money where is mouth is and he is not going to be willing to do that. How could he when he doesn't know?

Though your script has not told you this, there is a price to be paid in playing that game, and it is a terrible price. I am not just talking about time and money, though they will be costly enough. I am talking about the emotional price. I now need to turn to that.

Part III

The Price That Is To Be Paid for Legal Nonsense

CHAPTER 20

The Self-Fulfilling Prophecy

I want to go back to your script and ask a question. Where did it come from? After all, unlike the script to "Romeo and Juliet," you did not go out to a bookstore and buy it. You didn't have to. It was there just for the asking. As I said, it was "in the air." Thus, it wasn't necessary to purchase it in order for you to learn your lines. You knew them by heart. Though you were not aware of it, you had been programmed in advance to play your part.

Nevertheless, your script had to come from somewhere. As I said earlier, it was given to you by our adversarial legal system. Therein lies the problem. It mirrors a divorce lawyer's picture of the world of divorce and with it all of the assumptions that give silent support to that picture. Unfortunately, it is a very distorted picture, which is why it is not only going to get you into a lot of trouble but also require you to pay a terrible price.

To be sure, the script starts out simply enough. It tells you that, because you are divorcing, you have a legal problem. Moreover, you devoutly believe this, which is why one of your first thoughts was to turn to a lawyer. Unfortunately, it does not end that simply. Rather, following that script will make adversaries of you. That is how it always ends.

Why did we create an adversarial legal system? Why didn't we create a friendly system? I am not going to get into that. Suffice it to say that it is not a very friendly system, as anyone who has made the mistake of turning to it will tell you. In fact, that may be why you are reading this book. You have seen what happened to friends and relatives of yours who made the mistake of turning their lives over to lawyers. They seemed like fairly reasonable people just a few months ago. But since then all hell has broken loose. You do not want that to happen to you.

What does it mean to say that ours is an adversarial legal system? It means that, unlike Mark and Susan, who went off together to one lawyer, that is not what your script has instructed you to do. Since it reflects our adversarial legal system's view of divorce, it insists that you must each go off to separate lawyers. In fact, unlike Justin Wright, an adversarial divorce lawyer would not be willing to meet with the two of you.

Needless to say, there is no other time in your lives when you would have thought to do anything as unnatural as this. Nor would anyone have suggested it to you. You certainly did not do that when you decided to buy a home. To be sure, there were legal implications in that decision as well. But that didn't mean that you each went out and hired separate lawyers to represent you. What would have been the point of that? Rather, you went off together to one lawyer.

The same was true when one of your children developed a medical problem. Again, that required expert knowledge that neither of you possessed, which is why you consulted with a physician. But the two of you went off together to one physician to get her opinion and seek her advice. To be sure, you may have decided to get a second opinion. But you did that together as well.

Why should it be any different now? If the two of you have legal questions that you need answers to, and if your common sense tells you that you should go off together to one lawyer to get those answers as you always have in the past, why wouldn't you do that? There is no reason not to. Nevertheless, if you are like most divorcing husbands and wives, it would never occur to you to do that, which proves just how powerful your script is. No one told you that you each had to go off to separate lawyers. No one had to. You knew it without being told. In fact, it would never occur to you to bring your husband or wife with you when you go off to meet with an attorney and ask your questions. The script that you are blindly following has not programmed you to do that. It has programmed you not even to think of doing that, which is why it never occurred to you.

What reason has your script given you to do something now that you would never have thought to do at any other time in your life? In my terms, what is the justification for your doing something that is not only unnatural but also violates everything that your common sense would tell you. It is the assumption that the two of you are adversaries. To be sure, a divorce lawyer never insisted that the two of you were adversaries in your marriage. That is why he would never have suggested that there was anything inappropriate in your going off together to one lawyer to get whatever information or expert opinion you needed in the past. In fact, he would have felt very uncomfortable suggesting that you had to go off to separate lawyers. He doesn't feel uncomfortable suggesting that now, however. That is because, even if the two of you were not adversaries before, as far as a divorce lawyer is concerned, the minute you decide to divorce, that is what you become.

But aren't the two of you adversaries as divorce lawyers insist? It makes no difference. If you follow the script you have been given, that is exactly what you will become. Though you do not appreciate this as you should, our adversarial legal system proceeds on the basis of a self-fulfilling prophecy which, as you know, is something that becomes true because you assume it to be true. In other words, whether the two of you really are adversaries, whether you wish to be, or whether it even makes any sense for you to be, in assuming that you are adversaries, and then in organizing you as adversaries, that is exactly what you will become. In fact, the self-fulfilling prophecy works so effectively that, even though you do not know this, the two of you will become adversaries the minute one of you walks into your attorney's office. That is all it takes.

Let me explain this. Needless to say, neither you nor your husband or wife is going to make a public announcement that it is your intention to go off and meet with an attorney. Nor is either of you going to invite the other to come along with you when you do. Rather, you are going to go off and meet with your attorney on your own. In other words, you are going to meet with him secretly, privately, behind closed doors. And your husband or wife is going to do the same thing. That is what I meant when I said that our adversarial legal system is going to organize you as adversaries.

That is not how Mark and Susan met with Justin Wright, however. In other words, they were not organized as adversaries. Nor did they become adversaries the minute they walked into his office. As I characterize it, they met with him together, with their hands on top of the table. Neither of them had to worry what took place at the previous meeting when they were not there. Since Justin Wright would not have met with them separately, there was no such meeting. If one of them asked him a question, he wanted the other to be there to hear the answer. As I said, it was hands on top of the table.

That is not how you will be organized if you go off to separate lawyers, however. It will not be hands on top of the table. It will be hands under the table, and even if your hands are not doing anything, it is still going to make the other very uncomfortable. That is how it always starts. That is also all that is necessary. The self-fulfilling prophecy will do the rest.

CHAPTER 21

The Perfect Storm

As we have seen, divorcing husbands and wives run off blindly and turn their lives over to lawyers because their script tells them they have a legal problem. That being the case, they are no longer qualified to make the decisions in their lives. Only lawyers are. Again, although that was not the case in their marriage, it is now in their divorce. At least that is what their script would have them believe.

While that may tell you why you must turn to lawyers, it doesn't tell you why you must turn to separate lawyers. What justification does your script give you for this? There are two, and they are both very strange. The first is that the two of you have what our adversarial legal system characterizes as conflicting interests. The second, which is even stranger, is that lawyers are going to protect you. I will take up the question of your supposed conflicting interests at a later point. For the time being I want to address the second, namely, that lawyers are somehow going to protect you. You thought that lawyers were in one business, namely, to provide you with answers to your questions. As it turns out, they are in another. They are in the business of protection.

Understandably, like most husbands and wives who suddenly find themselves faced with the prospect of their divorce and the fact that they are going to be going forward pretty much on their own, you cannot help but be somewhat fearful and overwhelmed by a sense of anxiety. It is this that leaves you feeling that you are in danger and in need of protection. It is this that causes you to follow your script and run off to a lawyer. Your script would have you believe that doing that is nothing more than common sense. It would also have you believe that it is what I have characterized as legal sense.

It isn't. It is nothing but legal nonsense. As you will find if the two of you make the mistake of running off to lawyers for protection, it is dangerous nonsense as well. Contrary to what your script would have you believe, your separate lawyers are not going to protect you. Rather, all that they are going to do is create a situation which will put you in need of protection.

Let me explain this. What I am going to argue is that adversarial divorce proceedings create a perfect storm. Worse, once it has started, there is no way to stop it. That is because it quickly develops a life of its own. I could give a hundred examples to show this. One will suffice.

Following your script, you go off on your own and consult with an attorney. Your husband or wife is not your sworn enemy. Nor are you in mortal danger for your life. Whatever your problems may be, that is not the kind of protection you need. In fact, you have not really given very much thought as to why you are going off to a lawyer in the first place. That is just what your script has told you to do and, being understandably somewhat overwhelmed and more than a little nervous, that is what you are doing, though you would be hard pressed to say why if someone were to ask you.

When you got to your attorney's office, and in the course of your initial discussions with him, the fact that you and your husband had a joint savings account came up. "That's a problem," your attorney said. Before you had an opportunity to ask him why that was a problem, he went on. "You must go to the bank, withdraw all of the money in that account, and close it out. And you must do that immediately." Although he did not say this in so many words, it was understood that you were not to tell your husband of your intentions. You were just to go the bank and close out the account.

Understandably, that posed a problem for you. That is not how you normally conducted yourself—went out behind your husband's back and cleaned out your and his joint savings account. After all, you aren't a thief. Nevertheless, that is what you felt you were going to be if you followed your attorney's advice. And it didn't sit too well with you. In fact, it made you very uncomfortable.

When you told your attorney this, he smiled. "You and your husband are planning to divorce. Just as you are meeting with me, I have to assume that he will meet with an attorney as well. What is his attorney going to tell him? Leave the money in the account so that you can take it out? I don't think so. That leaves you with a choice. You can either be left a thief with the money or a fool without it. Which do you prefer?" Well, you would prefer neither, but the way that your attorney presented it to you, those seemed to be your only choices.

Why have you consulted with an attorney if you are not going to follow his advice? Besides, if you did not feel in danger and in need of protection when you entered his (or her) office, you certainly did by the time you left. The entire discussion was unsettling. All that you did was go there to ask some questions and get some answers. However, within almost no time the discussions had taken on a very different character. In fact, one of the things that you later asked yourself was why you found yourself angrier at your husband when you left your attorney's office than you were when you got there.

Nevertheless, your attorney was very emphatic. As he said, "This is not a tea party. You have witnessed what happened to friends and relatives of yours when they went through their own divorce. You have seen what their husbands did. You don't want that to happen to you. You have to protect yourself." And so you followed his advice, went to the bank and withdrew the money.

What was your husband's reaction when he found out that you had emptied the joint bank account? Did he understand that you were just trying to protect yourself? Did he pass it off by saying that all you were doing was following your attorney's advice? The question is a rhetorical one. He viewed it as a sneak attack on Pearl Harbor. Instead of discussing this with him, you had declared war by going out and dropping a bomb. Now all bets were off.

More than a little upset by all of this, you went back to your attorney, told him what your husband's reaction had been, and suggested that perhaps you should take half of the money you withdrew from the joint account and redeposit it into an account in his name alone. "I told you that this was not a tea party," your attorney replied. "I warned you how your husband was going to act. You just didn't believe me. Now you know for yourself that I was right"

Well you didn't know that. In fact, you never would. That is because your attorney's advice caused you to enact out a self-fulfilling prophecy. You may not have needed protection before you followed his advice. You certainly did now, however. That is the thanks that you got when you followed your script. It is the same thanks that every divorcing husband and wife gets when, making the mistake of assuming that they are somehow in danger, they allow themselves to enact out the self-fulfilling prophecy that then causes them to need protection.

I appreciate that it might be argued that the example I gave was an extreme one. It wasn't. But it makes no difference. If you follow your script, the two of you are each going to go off on your own. As I characterized it earlier, you are going to meet with your hands under the table, not in full view on top of the table. You are also each going to resort to self-help. After all, it is each man and woman for themselves.

That is where the perfect storm comes into play. Inevitably, in the atmosphere that will soon develop, each of you is going to say and do things that the other will consider to be inappropriate and take exception to. They may even view it as being adversarial. After all, that is what you are engaged in, an adversarial divorce proceeding. For everything said there will be a reply. For every action there will be a reaction. For every tit there will be a tat. It will make no difference how small what was said or done is. In time the vicious cycle of action and reaction will mushroom and get bigger and bigger. In time it will become a perfect storm. Worse, once it has been unleashed, there will be no way to stop it. There never is. That is because it will take on a life of its own. As I said, having followed your script and bought into the legal nonsense that lawyers are going to protect you, you are now both going to find yourself in need of protection. That is always how it begins. That is always how it ends.

That is not what happens when divorcing husbands and wives use their common sense and go off to a lawyer together. Neither of them has to worry what the other is doing. They know. They are doing it together. As I characterized it before, it is hands on top of the table.

There is a term for this. The term is context, and context is everything. To be sure, context will not change a lion into a lamb. But even lions and lambs act differently in different contexts. The two of you will as well. If you put yourselves in the context that the script you are following insists you must, go off to separate lawyers and deal with one another with your hands under the table, within no time at all you will have created the perfect storm. You don't have to take my word for it. All that you have to do is look at what happened to friends and relatives of yours who made that mistake.

If you put yourselves in a different context, your common sense is enough to tell you that this will not happen. But do not take my word for it. Again, all that you have to do is ask friends and relatives of yours who dealt with one another with their hands on top of the table. They will tell you.

CHAPTER 22

Bad Faith

I said that the attorney with whom you consult may tell you that it is not possible for him to answer your questions, at least as you would like to have them answered, when you first meet with him. He will tell you that he first needs to do his homework and get to know your case better. I want to assume that this is one of those situations in which this is true. Nevertheless, you have been led to believe that, after he has done his homework, he will then be able to answer your questions. Though you do not know this, he isn't going to do that. At least he isn't going to answer your questions with numbers that you could take to the bank. He isn't going to do that because he doesn't know the answers. As I said, a legal answer is not there just for the asking. It is the endpoint of a process, and your attorney and your husband's or wife's attorney will have very different opinions as to what those answers should be.

Ironically, it isn't going to make any difference that your attorney is not going to answer your questions. Once the game gets under way, and once you begin to get a little better understanding of how it is played, you will stop asking the questions that you originally did.

I appreciate that this may seem difficult to understand. You may even be offended by it. After all, you asked the questions that you did for a reason. Why will that reason be any less important tomorrow than it is today? It won't be. Nevertheless, you will stop asking those questions anyway. Something will have happened that will cause them not to seem as relevant. I already gave you part of the reason when I discussed what I characterized as the self-fulfilling prophecy and the perfect storm. But it goes beyond that. It is the malignancy that sets in and infects the entire atmosphere when husbands and wives take in too much of their script. To be sure, it starts in small ways and with little things. In almost no time, however, it will spread and ultimately infect the entire body of your relationship. I refer to it as bad faith. It is critical that you understand it.

You and your husband or wife have obviously talked with one another during your marriage. How else did you decide things? It is no less understandable that the two of you would talk (discuss things) now. After all, there are many things that the two of you have to decide, and it is the long way around to get to Cincinnati to have to discuss all of these things through your respective attorneys. It is also very expensive. Besides, do your attorneys really care that the two of you sat down and decided that your children will be returned on Sunday night before dinner rather than after dinner?

They don't care. Nevertheless, as strange as this may seem, your attorney will feel much more comfortable if you do not discuss anything with your husband or wife. In fact, that is going to be one of the first things that your attorney will tell you. You should let him do all of the talking. After all, that is what you are paying him to do.

Why does your attorney care whether you sit down with your husband or wife and decide when your children will be returned on Sunday night? As I said, he doesn't. Why, then, does he have a problem with this? Because he does not know where the discussion will lead. It may get into what is going to happen to your home. It may even get into the gift of $100,000 that Susan received and used to buy the home, and he does not want that. Better to instruct you not to discuss anything with your husband or wife. Better not to take any chances or assume any risk.

As you will find, attorneys have a very strange attitude when it comes to risk. That is because they are color blind when it comes to risk. While they see and are almost obsessed by certain risks, they are completely oblivious to others. Thus, though your attorney sees the risk involved in your discussing these things on your own with your husband or wife, he doesn't see the risk involved in sending out a message to your husband or wife that talking with them about anything other than the weather or what you are going to have for dinner is off limits.

But suppose that it would not get to that. Suppose you assure your attorney that you will not discuss anything with your husband or wife other than your children. What is the danger in that? After all, we already decided that your attorney could not care less whether your children are returned before dinner or after dinner on Sunday night. Nevertheless, he would still prefer that you not discuss anything with your husband or wife. Why?

It has to do with the game that the two of you are playing. To be sure, you may not be aware you are playing a game, but you are. It is a game of legal chess, and you do not give anything away, even a lowly pawn, for nothing. As your attorney knows from experience, you may need it as a bargaining chip for something else at a later point in time. That is why Mark's attorney didn't see any point in acknowledging what he knew, namely, that Susan was going to get back the $100,000 that she used to buy their home.

But certainly your attorney does not intend to use your children as bargaining chips, and he would be more than a little taken aback were someone to suggest that. Nevertheless, he doesn't know that your husband or wife might not do that, and he can't take any chances. He has played this game many times before, and he knows how it is played. He also knows that there are those who play it down and dirty, and he can't afford to take any chances. Besides, he remembers what Jack Nicholson said in reply to Shirley MacLaine in the movie "Terms of Endearment," and it is his watchword. Jack Nicholson was a former astronaut. To impress young women whom he was trying to seduce, he would take them into the trophy room in his house and show off all of the trophies and awards that he had received and won as an astronaut. When Shirley MacLaine chided him, and took him to task for what she considered to be his juvenile conduct, he replied, "You use everything that you have, and sometimes that isn't even enough."

Your attorney doesn't have to be reminded of this. Unlike you, he has played this game before and he knows it all too well. That being the case, he would feel more comfortable if you didn't discuss anything with your husband or wife, even something as inconsequential as whether your children will be returned before dinner or after dinner on Sunday night.

What is the inevitable effect of this? It is what I have referred to as bad faith. Ours is an adversarial legal system. What that means is that it assumes that the two of you are adversaries. As such, your husband or wife is not to be trusted. Moreover, within almost no time your conduct will make it clear to them that you don't. What else does it mean to say that you cannot discuss anything with them, even the most seemingly inconsequential things? In no time it will develop into the malignancy that I have characterized as bad faith.

I do not want or need to get into all of the other ways in which what I have characterized as bad faith will develop and mushroom into a malignant cancer. Since my concern here is why you will stop asking your attorney the question that he originally postponed answering, I want to fast forward and get to the point when both of your attorneys have done their homework and completed their discovery and inspection.

At that point in time, each of your attorneys is going to set forth his demands, or as they will politely refer to them, their offers of settlement. These proposed settlements do not represent what either of your attorneys has actually told you that you can expect. As I said, they have not really answered your questions when it comes to that. Rather, they are proposals that they will make for negotiating purposes. Your attorney knows that your husband's or wife's attorney is not going to put his cards on the table. In other words, each knows that the other is just taking a position for bargaining purposes. That is how the game is played.

Unfortunately, though your attorneys know this, you don't. Thus you are going to take those bargaining positions literally, particularly the offer of settlement that has been made by your husband or wife. (It was really made by your husband's or wife's attorney, but you will not make that distinction.) And since that offer was for so much less or for so much more than that proposed by your attorney, you are going to view it as nothing less than insulting. You are going to consider that it was made in bad faith. How else could you possibly view it in light of your own attorney's offer of settlement, which you will take to have been made, not for negotiating purposes, but in good faith?

The point is that your focus will no longer be on the proposal that your attorney has made—in the terms here, the question that you originally asked your attorney, that he postponed answering. Your focus will be on the proposal that your husband or wife has made, which you cannot help but view as evidence of their bad faith. In fact, the whole body of your relationship will have become infected with the malignancy of bad faith. That is what will make your original question irrelevant. It will no longer have anything to do with what is going on between the two of you and your respective attorneys.

CHAPTER 23

Feelings

I have already indicated one of the two principal reasons why divorcing husbands and wives make the mistake of following the script they have been given. It is the fear that they experience, and that understandably tends to overwhelm them, when they suddenly find themselves faced with the prospect of their divorce. Their script would have them believe that the reason they are in danger and in need of help is that they have unexpectedly wandered into uncharted legal waters. They feel that they are lost and adrift at sea and do not know in which direction to turn. That is why they must turn to lawyers, as it is only a lawyer who is qualified to navigate them through these dangerous waters.

Though the script that you have been given would lead you to believe this is nothing but legal sense, it isn't. It is simply legal nonsense. As should be clear by now, turning to divorce lawyers and our adversarial legal system is not going to protect you. It is going to have just the opposite effect. As the King of Siam famously put it, the only protection that you will get is to be protected out of everything you own.

There is another reason why divorcing husbands and wives make the mistake of following the script they have been given. It has to do with the feelings that are necessarily attendant to their divorce.

People do not get married to get divorced. This is not where they intended to be, nor is it where they feel they deserve to be. Rather, they feel that they are where they are because of something that the other has done or been unwilling to do. And since this is not where they intended to be or feel that they deserve to be, they cannot help but feel that what they have been made to suffer is a terrible injustice. And if an injustice has been done, someone should pay for it.

While this is understandable, it is nevertheless unrealistic. A divorce is not a morality play. It is not about punishing the guilty party and rewarding the innocent one. It is about ending a marriage. Admittedly, their script has not said anything to the contrary in so many words. Nevertheless, it has encouraged them to believe that this too is one of the objects of the procedure that they are being encouraged to employ to conclude their marriage.

That is where the lofty abstractions that divorce lawyers employ to characterize the undertaking come in. Again, divorce lawyers may not say this in so many words. Nevertheless, what divorcing husbands and wives interpret all of the talk about protecting their legal rights and securing an agreement that is fair and equitable to be saying is that, while your marriage may not have been fair, your divorce should be, as if their marriage and divorce take place in different worlds.

Again, this does not represent legal sense. It is simply legal nonsense. It is going to send you off on a fool's errand. Your husband or wife is the same person in your divorce that he or she was in your marriage. More to the point, whatever skills and ability a divorce lawyer may have, the one thing that he cannot do is make of your husband or wife in your divorce the person that you felt they never were in your marriage.

For better or worse, your husband or wife is your reality. As you had to deal with that reality in your marriage, so too will you have to deal with it in your divorce. The only question is how you will deal with it.

Your script would have you believe that the way to deal with it is to go toe-to-toe with your husband or wife, which is exactly what you will be doing if, following its instructions, you go off to separate lawyers. This does not represent legal sense. It is nothing but legal nonsense.

You have seen what has happened to husbands and wives who made the mistake of going off and doing legal battle with one another. You don't want the same fate for yourself. Your divorce will be difficult enough as it is. There is no point in making it more difficult. Again, your common sense is enough to tell you this.

Part IV

Substituting Your Common Sense for Legal Nonsense

CHAPTER 24

A Difference of Opinion

I now want to address the second justification that your script has given you for its insistence that you must each turn to separate lawyers rather than go off together to one lawyer. With that in mind, let me return to Mark and Susan and their grandfather clock. They have a difference of opinion when it comes to what should be done with it. Mark feels that he should keep it, Susan feels that she should. That is their problem.

What should they do? To be sure, their grandfather clock is important to both of them. But not so important that they should go to war over it. It would be better to give it to charity than to do that. There are other things that they could do as well. One would be to resort to my coin, which would also be a far better solution than going to war over it. Their common sense is enough to tell them that.

But while their common sense may be sufficient to tell them that they should not make this bigger than it is, it may not be enough to solve their problem. In fact, it may only leave them running around in circles with their differences of opinion. Thus, they are going to have to look to something. As I said, the only place that they can turn to is the law. Not because the law will give them the right answer. How could it possibly do that? Because it will at least give them an answer and, in doing that, hopefully end their problem.

How are they going to get an answer that will do that? Not by following their script and going off to separate lawyers. All that will accomplish will be to leave them with different answers—different legal opinions. They will only end up substituting their attorneys' difference of opinion for their own. What help will that have been? None. There is only one way to avoid that. That is to go off together to one lawyer. Since they will be getting the answer from the same lawyer, it will be the same answer.

Needless to say, that is not what your script has instructed you to do. Rather, it has told you that, whatever you do, you must not do that. Instead, you must go off to separate lawyers. There are supposedly two reasons for this. The first is that separate lawyers are somehow going to protect you. As we have already seen, this is nothing more than legal nonsense. In committing yourselves to do legal battle with one another, all that you will do is put yourselves in need of protection. It is now necessary to turn to the second reason.

Obviously, it will not do for your script to characterize the problems that the two of you will find yourselves faced with as being simply a difference of opinion. No one would suggest that it makes sense for the two of you to go off and do legal battle with one another over a mere difference of opinion. Thus, if your script is going to persuade you to do something as foolish and irresponsible as that, it will have to add more weight to that suggestion.

It does this by inflating what is at issue between the two of you. It does not say that you must look to the law because your common sense will not be sufficient. It says that you must look to the law because the law represents your legal rights. In the terms that I have put it, it says that the law trumps your common sense. More importantly, it does not characterize the two of you, as I have, as simply having a difference of opinion. It characterizes the two of you as having what a divorce lawyer refers to as conflicting interests. I have already dealt with the first of these justifications. I now need to address the second.

When divorce lawyers say that divorcing husbands and wives have conflicting interests, they talk as if they are saying something very profound. In other words, they talk as if there is nothing further that needs to be said. The two of you have conflicting interests and your conflicting interests militate that you must get the answers to your questions from separate attorneys. That is all there is to it.

No it isn't. In fact, despite what divorce lawyers believe, and despite what your script has told you, nothing follows from the fact that the two of you have what our adversarial legal system chooses to characterize as conflicting interests. After all, your supposed conflicting interests do not come with a set of instructions telling you what you should do with them—applaud them or laugh at them, encourage them or discourage them, champion them or, instead, resolve them. It is only our adversarial legal system that arbitrarily and gratuitously insists that there is only one thing that you can do with them, and that is to go off and do legal battle in their name.

I have suggested that the two of you have a difference of opinion. Divorce lawyers insist that the two of you have conflicting interests. We are both obviously looking at the same thing. We are just describing it differently. But what difference does the difference in our descriptions make? In other words, when all is said and done, what is its cash value? After all, as Shakespeare reminded us, a rose by any other name would smell the same.

That may be true when it comes to names. It is not necessarily true, however, when it comes to characterizations. Names are always passive. They do not do anything or go anywhere. Characterizations, however, are not always passive. More often than not, they are active. They prompt us into action. That is why our favorite characterizations are so important to us, at least if they are active. They cause people to act in a certain way—as we would like them to act.

This would be apparent if our adversarial legal system characterized divorcing husbands and wives as being "in conflict" (an active characterization) rather than as "having conflicting interests" (a passive characterization). The first characterization, being active, would cause us to ask questions and to make judgments that the second, being passive, does not.

Let me explain this. No responsible person would suggest that we should increase the conflict that we find in the world. On the contrary, we would want to resolve it, or at least decrease it. Thus, if two people are "inconflict," and if it is proposed that they should act in a certain manner, or that we should intervene in a particular way, the question that we will naturally ask is whether the proposed conduct or intervention will tend to decrease their conflict, and possibly resolve it or, instead, aggravate it and thereby increase it. After all, the reason why we are proposing the action or intervention in the first place is to be of help.

The same is not true of the characterization "conflicting interests," however. It is more a statement of fact, which is why I have described it as being passive. It is like saying that one of them has blue eyes and the other brown eyes. Nothing necessarily follows from that fact (characterization). In other words, it does not tell us how to react or what to do. That is why our adversarial legal system employs that characterization. Since it is a blank slate, it allows it to put whatever label (set of instructions) on it that it wants to—in this case, that the two of them must each retain separate lawyers and go off and do legal battle with one another. If divorce lawyers say this often enough and long enough, we will soon forget that its characterization did not come packaged with those instructions. Instead, we will come to believe that they represent the only conclusion that could possibly follow from that characterization.

The same would not be true if our adversarial legal system's characterization of divorcing husbands and wives was that they are "in conflict." Since that is an active characterization, not a passive one, rather than give our adversarial legal system a blank slate on which to write any instructions it wishes, it would cause us to ask all of the questions that our adversarial legal system's characterization tends to mute. Thus, we would ask whether a particular set of instructions—a particular proposed course of action—will tend to increase or decrease their conflict. After all, who would recommend that we do anything to increase it. Ironically, although you are not supposed to see this, that is exactly what the set of instructions that our adversarial legal system would have you follow will necessarily do. As I said, in assuming that you are adversaries, it is going to make adversaries of you.

This is where the range of possible answers that you are going to be left with if you follow the script that you have been given comes in. Based on our adversarial legal system's characterization of your problem—that the two of you have, not a difference of opinion, but conflicting interests—it insists that you must go off to separate lawyers to get the answers to your questions. What that means, of course, is that, since the application of legal rules cannot leave you with just one answer, but only a range of possible answers, you are necessarily going to come back with different answers. But that is only part of the problem. The other part is that going to separate lawyers can only have one effect, which is to dramatically increase the size of that range of possible answers. As I characterized it, it will not only leave you with different answers to the same question, but with answers that literally will not talk to one another.

What effect will that have? This is one of the things about adversarial divorce proceedings that you have not been told. You will not even find mention of it in the small print at the end of your script. It can only have one effect. Based on its characterization that the two of you have conflicting interests, our adversarial legal system insists that you must each go off to separate lawyers to get the answers to your questions. Going off to separate lawyers can only have one effect, which is to increase your conflict. As I said earlier, its effect will be to create the perfect storm.

The same will not be true if you disregard your script and go off together to the same lawyer. That is because you will both be given the same answers, not different ones. In my terms, regardless of how Mark and Susan may feel about their grandfather clock, if they are both given the same answer, they will have no choice but to assume that it is correct. Even if they still have different feelings about their grandfather clock, as they undoubtedly will, other considerations—in this case that we have been brought up to accept impartial judgments—will hopefully put the matter to rest. In other words, if they are both given the same answer, they will be under a lot of pressure to accept it.

It could be objected to that the example I have used is not an appropriate one. After all, many of the issues that you, like Mark and Susan, will have to resolve are far more important than their grandfather clock. Certainly that is the case when it comes to the issue of how much one of you should pay to the other for his or her support and for how long, one of you feeling that you should pay one amount for a certain period of time and the other feeling that you should receive a greater amount for a longer period of time. But the importance of the issue, and your different feelings about it, does not change the fact that what the two of you are left with is still only a difference of opinion. Characterizing it as your having conflicting interests doesn't change that. It just causes you to lose sight of it.

I want to carry the argument a little further. To do that, and for the sake of the argument, I want to accept that the two of you have what your script characterizes as conflicting interests. I will go even further and accept that what you have conflicting interests about is what divorce lawyers refer to as your legal rights. What difference does that make? After all, your difference of opinion (conflicting interests) is not an intellectual one. In other words, what you have a difference of opinion (conflicting interests) about is not what your legal rights are. Neither of you has an opinion here. How could you if have not gone to law school? It is about how you feel, one of you feeling that you should not be required to pay the other more than a certain amount for a certain period of time and other feeling that you should. Nor does characterizing this as representing conflicting interests change anything. It still leaves you with the same problem. And it still leaves you with the question of how you are going to resolve that conflict.

You only have two choices. You can go off together to one lawyer who will give you the same answer and, in doing that, hopefully help you solve your problem. Or, following the script that you have been given, you can go off to separate lawyers who, in giving you different answers to the same question, will only leave you with a problem. Again, it does not take a legal education to tell you which of these two choices makes more sense. All that you need is your common sense.

CHAPTER 25

Getting it Right—Getting it Done

Our adversarial legal system is grounded on an unbending principle. That principle is that the presence of conflicting interests militates separate representation. Nor are there any exceptions to this. That is why I refer to it as an unbending principle. Thus, the fact that the two of you have had a long relationship, have been married to one another, and may even have had children together, is irrelevant. The two of you have conflicting interests and you are therefore adversaries. That may not have been true in your marriage. Nevertheless, it becomes true the minute you decide to divorce. That is why your script insists that you must each consult with, and be represented by, separate lawyers.

Nevertheless, there is something very curious about our adversarial legal system's attitude when it comes to this principle. While it makes a big fuss about conflicting interests, it is also very selective when it comes to them. Sometimes it insists upon their importance and at other times it ignores them. In the terms that concern us here, it only recognizes external conflicts—the conflict that you have with one another. It completely ignores internal conflicts—the one that you are going to have with yourself.

Let me explain this. If you retain your own separate lawyer as your script insists you must, your lawyer will tell you that his object will be to negotiate an agreement on your behalf. The problem is that the two of you (actually your two lawyers) are going to have very different opinions when it comes to what that agreement should look like. That is what your attorneys mean when they say that the two of you have conflicting interests. It is also why, so our adversarial legal system insists, the two of you must each be represented by separate lawyers. There must always be separate representation when there is a conflict of interests.

Nevertheless, while your attorney will make a big to-do about the conflict that the two of you are going to have with one another, he will completely ignore the conflict that you are going to have with yourself. This is what I was referring to when I said that our adversarial legal system has very different attitudes when it comes to conflict, in this case external conflicts and internal conflicts. It makes a big fuss when it comes to one and completely ignores the other.

What is the internal conflict that you are inevitably going to experience? Part of you is going to want to get it right. Another part of you is going to want to get it done. This would not be a problem if your two attorneys agreed on what was right—in the terms that I have put it, if they both gave you the same answers to your questions. But they won't. Rather, as we have seen, they are going to have very different opinions as to what would pass that test. This would also not be a problem if the application of legal rules was able to leave you with clear answers to your questions. Regardless of what your separate attorneys thought was right, like the application of mathematical rules, the application of legal rules would decide the matter. But as we have seen, the application of legal rules will not leave you with clear answers to your questions. Rather, all that you will be left with is a range of possible answers and, if you follow the script you have been given and get those answers from different lawyers, a very large range at that. In other words, they will leave you where you started out, which is nowhere.

That is where your own internal conflict will come in. It is going to leave you with a very difficult choice. You can hold out in an attempt to get it right—to get what your lawyer will characterize as being an agreement that is fair and equitable. Unfortunately, that may take forever. Or you can settle the matter in order to get it done—be left with an agreement that your lawyer has characterized as being unfair and inequitable. That is going to be your dilemma. In my terms, that is going to be the internal conflict that you will find yourself having to struggle with.

Nor will this conflict be an imaginary one. As you will find, it is going to be very real. You have good reasons for not wanting it to take forever. After all, you need to get on with your life, and you are not going to be able to do that unless and until you get it done. That is why getting it done will be so important. By the same token, you do not want to get it wrong, which is what you will be afraid may happen if you settle the matter just to get it done. That will be the internal conflict you are going to experience.

Unfortunately, your script is going to make it very difficult for you to resolve the conflict. That is because it has misled you into believing that there not only is a right answer, but then prejudiced the matter further by magnifying the importance of getting that answer. It has done so by characterizing it as representing, not simply the answer that you would get if the question was decided by the application of legal rules, but as your inalienable legal rights. In short it has loaded the dice against your being able get it done. It has persuaded you that if you do not hold out to get it right, you are going to get it wrong and be left a fool. Needless to say, no one wants to be left a fool.

This brings us back to our legal system's unbending principle. If our adversarial legal system really meant it when it said that the presence of conflicting interests militated separate representation, since you are clearly going to be left with a conflict, and since it has been established that one lawyer cannot represent both sides of a conflict, your script should insist that you must have two attorneys, one to advocate on behalf of your getting it right and the other on behalf of your getting it done.

Needless to say, our adversarial legal system does not carry its cardinal principle that far. As I said, it is very selective when it comes to conflicting interests. Sometimes it recognizes them, other times it completely ignores them.

But our adversarial legal system does more than ignore one of your important interests, namely, to get it done. It allows a divorce lawyer to do the very thing it insists he may not do, which is to enter the lists and champion one of your two conflicting interests, to get it right, at the expense of the other, to get it done. To be sure, it does not say this in so many words. Nevertheless, that is what it does.

That, again, is where the lofty abstractions that divorce lawyers forever invoke—*legal rights, fair* and *equitable*—come in. When they were invoked in the name of equity, their effect was to disable you from being able to see that the application of legal rules would not leave you with any answers to your questions, let alone the right one. When they are now invoked in the name of getting it right, their effect will be to disable you from being able to see that they will stand in the way of your getting it done. In fact, in entering the lists as a champion for one of your two interests—in a divorce lawyer's terms, securing your legal rights—your other important interest, getting it done, will soon become all but irrelevant.

To be sure, a divorce lawyer would take exception to this. He would insist that he too is anxious to get it done—as he characterizes it, to conclude an agreement. In fact, in support of this, he would boast that probably no more than five or at the most ten percent of his cases are resolved by a trial. That, so he would argue, is not only proof of his commitment to getting it done but also evidence of his skill in being able to accomplish this.

Again, this is simply legal nonsense. Your attorney's skill will have nothing to do with it. The truth is that, finally, when you are emotionally and financially exhausted, and when your only other choice is a long and costly trial, you will give up and give in. You will agree to "settle" the matter, which is a divorce lawyer's polite way to say that one of you will either accept less or give more than you were led to believe you were legally entitled or obligated to.

In other words, characterizing your differences as conflicting interests rather than a difference of opinion isn't going to change anything. It certainly isn't going to solve your problems. In enacting out the self-fulling prophecy that I described, all that it is going to do is make it that much more difficult for the two of you to bring the matter to an end. As I said, that does not represent legal sense. It is legal nonsense, and all of the lofty abstractions in the world will not change that. Their only effect will be to disable you from being able to see it. But, then, that is why divorce lawyers forever invoke them.

CHAPTER 26

Beating the Game—Beating the System

Though your script has told you that it is essential that you make what it describes as informed, intelligent decisions, and though you have been told that the only way to do that is to consult with a lawyer who is expert in these matters to get answers to your questions, you could not possibly do that. How could you when the procedure that you have been instructed to employ is nothing more than a game? How could you when that game has literally been designed to prevent you from getting reliable answers to your questions—in the terms here, to make an informed, intelligent decision?

Where does that leave you? Put another way, how do you get out of the dilemma that your script has left you with? One way would be to beat the game. How could you do that? Let's consider that.

When you go off to separate lawyers, you know that you are each going to be given different answers to the same question. In my terms, you are each going to be shown a very different portion of the range of possible answers, the portion most favorable to you. The problem is that neither of you will hear or see what the other has been told or shown. That is how the game is played.

How could you beat the game? The easiest way would be to bring your husband or wife along with you when you go and consult with an attorney. And your husband or wife could do the same. The necessary effect of that would be to assure that you will both hear the whole story—in the terms here, that you will both get a picture of the entire range of possible answers rather than a narrow, distorted picture. It would also assure that you will both be given the same answers to your questions rather than different ones. If making an informed, intelligent decision really means knowing what the legal answers to your questions are, that would put you in a position to do that.

As we have already seen, no adversarial divorce lawyer is going to be willing to allow you to do this. It is not just that it would give away the game—show you how the game is played. It is that if each of you were given this opportunity, you would never be willing to play the game. The game only works when neither of you is allowed to see what takes place when the other meets with his or her attorney.

How will an adversarial divorce lawyer excuse his not being willing to do this? He will play the game. Falling back on the rules of the game, he will say that it would be unethical for him to meet with your husband or wife. He can only meet with you alone.

Ironically, that is a very curious answer. Why, after all, is your attorney telling you what your legal rights are—in the terms here, what your husband's or wife's obligation is? Not for your benefit. (It isn't important that you know what they are obligated to do.) It is for their benefit. (It is important that they know.) Nevertheless, as important as it is that your husband or wife know what your legal rights are, the rules of the game are that your attorney is not allowed to tell them. That is why I said that the answer (really excuse) that you will be given is a very curious one.

If none of this squares with your common sense, there is a reason for it. It violates everything that your common sense would tell you. Our adversarial legal system insists that it would be unethical for one lawyer to meet with the two of you and give you a picture of the whole range of possible answers. To be sure, divorce lawyers may characterize this in ethical terms. But that does not change anything. Nor does it constitute legal sense, as they would have you believe. It is still nothing but legal nonsense.

Notwithstanding what our adversarial legal system may say, it could not possibly be inappropriate for one lawyer to meet with the two of you and give you an objective picture of the range of possible answers. What is inappropriate, and in fact irresponsible, is for a divorce lawyer to meet with only one of you and give you a narrow, and therefore distorted, picture of the range of possible answers. What is worse is his expressing an opinion when he has only heard half of the story rather than the whole story—the half that you have told him but not the half that your husband or wife would tell him if they had been given the opportunity. But I am being too polite. I should put it in the terms that your script insists upon. It is unethical.

Where does that leave you? It leaves you with your other possible choice. If you can't beat the game, your only other choice is to beat the system. How can you do that? Ironically, it is very simple. Don't play the game. Throw your script in the garbage can, where it belongs. If you want to be given the same answers to your questions rather than different ones, you are going to have to go off together to the same lawyer to get them. To be sure, that is not what your script has told you. Nevertheless, it is what your common sense would tell you if you would only listen to it.

There is another reason why you shouldn't play the game. You are going to pay a terrible price if you do. I am not just talking about money, though it will certainly be costly in that way as well. If you are not careful, it could cost a king's ransom. I am talking about how it is going to make it even more difficult for the two of you to conclude an agreement than I have already indicated. I am talking about how it is going to take what is already a tragedy in your lives and turn it into a nightmare. To be sure, you will not find any mention of this in your script. Again, it would give away the game.

If you choose to beat the system and not play the game, does that mean that you will not need the help of a lawyer? I did not say that. You will. For better or worse, your common sense is only going to take you so far. You will need some help to take you the rest of the way. That is why you will turn to a lawyer and the law. You do not have any other place to turn.

But how will a lawyer's role be different if you don't play the game? I now need to turn to that.

CHAPTER 27

An Attorney and Counselor-At-Law

As we have seen, the script that you have been encouraged to follow has misled you in many ways. It has misled you in another way as well, and that is in suggesting that a lawyer only has one role. That is not true. He has two. Your script has just failed to mention the other. He is an attorney and he is a counselor-at-law. A lawyer does not generally perform both of these roles at the same time. Sometimes he only performs one. That is true of a divorce lawyer. He is always an attorney.

An attorney is an advocate. He represents a client and his role is to advance his client's interests. The instrument that he will use for that purpose is the law. Since adversarial divorce proceedings are simply a form of legal combat, it would be more accurate to refer to the law as a weapon. Thus, though an attorney may say that the object of his efforts is simply to conclude an agreement that is fair and equitable, what he really wants, and what he is charged with the responsibility of doing, is to get what is best for his client. And what is best for his client? To get as much as he can and to give as little as he has to. In short, what he is engaged in is a game of legal chess and its object, as is the object in all games, is to win. But what about his client's husband or wife, or even their children? As I said, that is not an attorney's concern. In fact, it would be unethical for him to consider them.

A counselor-at-law will look to the law differently. He is not playing a game. He is trying to solve a problem. Since he is working with two people, as was the case when Mark and Susan met with Justin Wright, his role will be very different. As Justice Louis Brandeis famously answered when he was asked who he represented when he helped two clients of his to work out a problem that they had, "I was the attorney for the situation."

Mark and Susan did not consult with Justin Wright to solve a problem just for one of them. They were certainly not trying to solve it for one of them at the expense of the other. What would have been the point of that? Rather, they were trying to solve it for both of them—in the context here, to conclude an agreement that they both felt they could live with. Their problem was that they were not able to do that on the basis of their common sense and the considerations that were important to the two of them alone. That is why they turned to the law. They were hoping that the law would be able to help them. To be sure, the law would not do that if all that it left them with were different answers to the same question, which is what would have happened had they followed their script and gone off to separate lawyers. It would, or at least might, if they went off to the same lawyer together, which is why they consulted with Justin Wright.

But aren't you, like Mark and Susan, going to have the same problem when you consult with one lawyer together? After all, as we have seen, in most instances at least, the application of legal rules will not leave you with one and only one answer. Rather, it will only leave you with a range of possible answers. Certainly that will be the case when it comes to the payment that one of you will make to the other for his or her support, and the amount and duration of that payment. Just as important, won't you have the same conflict in terms of your need to get it right and your desire to get it done whether you turn to separate lawyers or to one lawyer?

The answer is yes on both counts. But it is also no. Yes, you will still be left with a range of possible answers rather than just one answer regardless of which road you go down. Nevertheless, if you go off to one lawyer together, that may not pose the same insurmountable obstacle that it inevitably will if you follow the script that you have been given and turn to separate lawyers. To begin with, you will be given a picture of the whole range of possible answers, not just a small portion of it, that most favorable to you. Second, there will not be the tendency, inherent in an adversarial divorce proceeding, to increase the size of the range of possible answers to the point that they do not talk to one another. Rather, since a counselor-at-law's role will be different, the tendency will be to narrow the range of possible answers and, hopefully, leave you with answers that will talk to one another.

There is one last difference and it can make all of the difference. Unlike your separate attorneys, the one lawyer you meet with will not be advocating on behalf of either of the extremes of that range of possible answers. In fact, he will not be advocating at all. What would be the point of that? Rather, he will see his role to be to encourage the two of you to look at this for what it is, not as a morality play, as your separate attorneys would have it, but as a practical life problem, that problem being how each of you is going to be able to manage financially in the future and the obligation, if any, that one of you should have to the other to be concerned with how he or she will be able to do that. Characterizing all of this in terms of your legal rights and your conflicting interests, as your two attorneys will do, will not change that. It will just cause you to lose sight of it.

What about your other, internal conflict? Without question, you will still be left with it. You will want to get it right, but you will also want to get it done. Nevertheless, consulting with one lawyer together rather than with separate attorneys may possibly be helpful here as well. In that regard, it is important to keep in mind that there is not only a difference between an attorney's and a counselor-at-law's roles, there is also a difference in the settings in which they will perform those roles. In fact, as you will find if you decide not to play the game, those roles and settings will constitute a world of difference.

With that in mind, let us return to the internal conflict that you will have between getting it right and getting it done. The setting in which that conflict will play itself out if you follow your script and go off to separate lawyers can only have one effect on that conflict. That is to increase it. It is almost as if it has been designed with that in mind. That is because, the wider the range of possible answers, the wider will be the gap between getting it right and getting it done. Nor will there be any way to bridge it.

Turning to separate lawyers will increase that conflict in another way as well. As we have seen, it is in the very nature of an adversarial divorce proceeding, which will frame everything in terms of what it refers to as your legal rights, to privilege getting it right over getting it done. That might be acceptable if your two attorneys agreed on what was right. But they won't. Thus, if getting it right is that important, and if the application of legal rules will alone guarantee that, since a legal answer is not there just for the asking, there will be only one way for you to get it. You will have to play the game to the end. You will have to go off to the court of last resort to get it. You will have to go to trial.

That is the fool's errand that your script is going to send you on. Following it will not leave you with the right answer. There is no right answer. All that a court's decision will do is end the matter because the two of you were not smart enough and responsible enough to conclude it on your own. So you will lose on both counts if you follow your script. You won't get it right and you won't get it done.

That brings me to your other choice, which is not to play the game. I am not suggesting that going off to one lawyer together is necessarily guaranteed to solve all of your problems. Why then, am I recommending it?

I could say that you should do that because it is always how you dealt with questions that had to be answered or problems that had to be solved in the past. If you had a question that required expert opinion, you went off together to one professional. And that would be a good enough reason. But there is a better one.

I said that if your script is correct when it says that the two of you have a conflict, then in considering what course of action you should take, the appropriate question to ask is whether the one under consideration will tend to aggravate that conflict or, instead, assuage it. The course of action that your script recommends can only have one effect, which is to aggravate it. You don't need me to tell you that. You know it without my having to tell you.

The other course of action is not designed to have that effect. Its natural tendency will be just the opposite. That is because it will be hands on top of the table rather than hands under the table. More important, in leaving the two of you with the same answers to your questions, it will not have the effect of planting the seeds of bad faith that becomes so insidious in an adversarial divorce proceeding. But it will do something else. It will give you a safe place to work out what will inevitably be the necessary tension between your wanting to get it right and your need to get it done.

This again is where an attorney's and a counselor-at-law's different roles, and the different settings in which they work, come in. An attorney only meets with one of you. Since he does not see your husband or wife, it would be impossible for him to factor them into the equation. Besides, he is not ethically allowed to do that. His role is to be your advocate, and the natural effect of the setting in which he works tends to reinforce his role as such.

A counselor-at-law, on the other hand, will be meeting with the two of you. It is therefore not possible for him to see only one of you. More important, it would be an inconsistency in terms for him to act as one of your advocates. Who would be representing the other? Thus, just as an attorney's natural tendency will be to act as an advocate, a counselor-at-law's natural tendency will be to act as an intermediary.

But it goes beyond that. Unlike an attorney, who will answer your questions without any regard as to the effect that his answers will have on your husband or wife, a counselor-at-law will be very concerned with the effect that they will have. He is not just dispensing what he would refer to as legal information. He is trying to use the law as a means of helping the two of you resolve whatever differences of opinion are preventing you from concluding an agreement. Thus, it is not sufficient just to give you information about the law. It is also necessary to help you to accept it.

A counselor-at-law has many things going for him in that regard that an attorney does not. To begin with, he is mentally less restricted. An attorneys suffers from mental paralysis. His mind is only able to focus on what is legally relevant. It cannot bend to acknowledge what is personally relevant. A counselor-at-law does not suffer this same disability. In other words, since he does not sanctify the law, he is able to see legal rules for what they are, namely, arbitrary rules having little if anything to do with the realities of your lives. How could he see them as being anything but that when he knows, for example, that the law of Massachusetts would not credit Susan with the $100,000 gift that her father made to her. Unlike New York, where Mark and Susan happen to live, Massachusetts does not make the distinction between separate property and marital property. Everything goes into the pot. Everything is subject to distribution.

To be sure, a counselor-at-law will not get into all of this with them. It would only confuse them. It would confuse them even more if he told them that even in New York, if their marriage had ended as the result of Susan's death rather than their divorce, Mark, would have been entitled to share in the gift that her father had made to her. Unlike its divorce laws, New York's estate laws do not make the distinction between separate property and marital property either. Like Massachusetts, everything goes into the pot, which is what I mean when I say that legal rules are simply arbitrary rules having little if anything to do with the realities of your lives.

The point is that, though a counselor-at-law may not get into all of this with Susan and Mark, he knows that there is a difference between legal relevance and personal relevance. The fact that Mark's argument may not be legally relevant doesn't mean that it is not personally relevant. In fact, it makes a lot of sense, even if Susan's lawyer, whose mental paralysis will only allow him to acknowledge what is legally relevant, will not think so. And in the setting in which a counselor-at-law will work with the two of them, Mark will be able to express how he feels. Nor will anyone tell him he is a fool just because a court in New York (in their divorce but not in their marriage) will not deem his feelings to be relevant.

That can make all of the difference. Perhaps now that he has been heard, Mark will be able to say that Susan can keep the $100,000 that was given to her by her father. Perhaps having been given an opportunity to hear how Mark feels, and to acknowledge the validity of how he feels, Susan will be able to say that she will share all or a portion of that gift with Mark, just as he shared other things with her. These are not possibilities that are likely to arise in the setting in which the two of them will be placed if they play the game and go off to separate attorneys. As I said, it has almost been designed to exclude them as possibilities.

To be sure, it is possible that, having heard one another, they may still be left with a difference of opinion. If that is the case, at least if the law is clear and therefore makes legal sense in his terms, a counselor-at-law will try to get them to accept what the law considers to be legally relevant, even if one of them feels that it is not personally relevant. After all, there is no methodology to the application of their personal feelings either, and the object is to get it done. Besides, when all else fails, what the law considers to be relevant is a reality that they will have to live with whether or not it squares with what they consider to be personally relevant.

That is where a counselor-at-law's role as an intermediary comes in. Hopefully, if he is faithful to his role as a counselor-at-law, the two of them will come to trust him—in the context here, come to believe that he is trying to help the two of them, not just be the advocate for one of them. He in turn will be concerned not just with what he tells them, but also with how he tells it to them. In other words, unlike their separate attorneys, who will have absolutely no concern as to whether their client's husband or wife is able to hear or accept what they say, a counselor-at-law, acting as an intermediary, will be very concerned with this, which is why he will try to tell it in a way that will enable them to accept it. What value would it be otherwise?

That is going to make a world of difference. It is going to make a difference in another way as well. Acting as a counselor-at-law (an intermediary) rather than as an attorney (an advocate), he will help you come to terms with the reality that it is necessary to make compromise with life rather than make that more difficult. As we all know, a branch breaks where it cannot bend. That is why it is so important to be resilient.

That is not the counsel you will get if you follow the script that you have been given. It will tell you that you must be steadfast and unbending. Since it will characterize everything in terms of principle, it will even try to persuade you that doing that is a virtue. Being rigid is never a virtue. It is a failing.

CONCLUSION

Nothing that I have said is meant to suggest that deciding not to follow your script and play the game will solve all of your problems. That would be irresponsible. There are no magic elixirs. Nevertheless, how you choose to view your problem, and the context in which you attempt to deal with it, will make all the difference in the world.

As we have seen, you can view it as a legal problem or you can view it as a personal problem that simply has certain legal implications. If you do the former, you will make lawyers the experts in your lives and empower them to make all of the important decisions. You will allow impersonal legal rules to become the arbiter in your lives.

If you do the latter, lawyers will have a more limited role. You will make the decisions in your lives, just as you always have in the past, based on your good judgment and the personal considerations that are important to you. You will only turn to lawyers, and make those decisions based on the arbitrary legal rules that they employ, when you are unable to do that on your own.

Admittedly, there are no guarantees whatever you do. But there is still an important difference. Regardless of how it is packaged, viewing your problem as a legal problem, and following your script and turning to adversarial divorce proceedings, is only going to make it more difficult rather than less difficult for the two of you to solve your problems and conclude an agreement. How could it do anything other than that when what it is going to commit the two of you to is to do legal battle with one another? Divorce lawyers may try to persuade you that doing that makes legal sense. It doesn't. It is legal nonsense.

Turning to a lawyer who will act as a counselor-at-law and an intermediary will have a very different effect. To begin with, rather than reinforcing your inevitable fears and aggravating the difficult feelings that you are struggling with, the setting in which you will meet as I have put it, with your hands on top of the table rather than under the table will have just the opposite effect. Just as important, that setting will give you a safe place to work out the inevitable conflict that you will have between getting it right and getting it done.

To be sure, if you chose to view your problems in the way I am suggesting makes more sense, you will still be faced with how the two of you are going to resolve what will inevitably be your differences of opinion. But you will not solve that problem by following your script and going off to separate lawyers. In other words, you will have a problem whichever road you go down. Nevertheless, there is a difference. The road I am recommending may be a risk. The other is a certainty. And between a risk and a certainly, there can only be one choice.

But don't take my word for it. You must know husbands and wives who made the mistake of following the script they were given. Ask them if what I have told you is not the absolute truth. The irony is that you don't have to ask them. As everyone knows, the only thanks they got for their efforts was to be given false levels of expectation that were then inevitably followed by equivalent levels of disappointment. That is the sad legacy that our adversarial legal system has bequeathed to divorcing husbands and wives. You don't want it to be your legacy as well.

Made in the USA
Lexington, KY
19 August 2011